PAPERS
on
THE CONSTITUTION

George Washington at Princeton

The U.S. Army Bicentennial Series

PAPERS
on
THE CONSTITUTION

John W. Elsberg
General Editor

MILITARY INSTRUCTION

Center of Military History
United States Army
Washington, D.C., 1990

Foreword

One of the principal events in the Center's observation of the Bicentennial of the U.S. Constitution was a series of lectures delivered under the sponsorship of Secretary of the Army John O. Marsh, Jr., at Fort McNair. There, a group of eminent scholars reviewed for a select audience of military and academic leaders the role of the Framers in the formation of the new Republic. Their conclusions, always pertinent, often intriguing, were set forth in papers that rank with the finest in American scholarship.

As part of our intention to preserve what was best in our Army's celebration of the Bicentennial, we are publishing these lectures, along with two other papers on the Constitution, not only as a token of our commitment to the dissemination of this important scholarship to a wider military and public audience, but also as a further affirmation of the Army's enduring commitment to its primary responsibility, summarized in every soldier's oath, "to support the Constitution of the United States against all enemies, foreign and domestic; that I will bear true faith and allegiance to the same."

Washington, D.C.
8 February 1990

HAROLD W. NELSON
Colonel, USA
Chief of Military History

Preface

In September 1987 the United States commemorated the Bicentennial of the signing of the Constitution. The U.S. Army joined with the rest of the federal government and many cities and communities to celebrate the occasion with appropriate ceremony. The Army in particular had much to remember, since twenty-two of the thirty-nine men who signed the Constitution were Army veterans, men who had served under arms during the Revolutionary War. These old soldiers were patriots in every sense of that word. They had fought in various units and ranks for the cause of Independence; they signed the new Constitution as representatives of twelve of the thirteen states; and they then spent years helping to forge the new government, many going on to careers of distinguished public service during the critical formative years of the nation. They left a legacy of responsible leadership that has endured as a preeminent model through two hundred years of national development and change.

Under the guidance of Secretary John O. Marsh, Jr., the Army dedicated 1987 to the Constitution and to the memory of these Soldier-Statesmen of the Constitution. The goal was to remind every soldier of the lasting contribution made by these veterans of an earlier era to the cause of freedom and the establishment of an effective and equitable government by and for the people. In particular, the Secretary wanted to make clear to the men and women of today's Army that these Framers of the Constitution established for all time the precedent that the military, subordinated to Congress, would remain the servant of the Republic. As he reminded his audiences, this concept is the underpinning of the American military tradition—a tradition that is reaffirmed in a special way when, at the beginning of military service, each new soldier repeats the familiar words:

> I do solemnly swear (or affirm) that I will support the Constitution of the United States against all enemies, foreign and domestic; that I will bear true faith and allegiance to the same.

The Army's efforts in support of the Bicentennial of the Constitution took many different forms. But one program, the Bicentennial Lecture Series initiated by Secretary Marsh, perhaps made the most lasting contribution to original scholarly research and writing on the Constitution. With the advice of the Chief of Military History, Mr. Marsh invited six distinguished historians to lecture on the Constitution and on the men who devised it before an audience of senior Army leaders and scholars from the Washington, D.C., area in the hall of the venerable National Defense University building at Fort Leslie J. McNair. He also commissioned two related papers to complement these lectures. With a general focus, to provide a broad context, these lectures and papers ranged across the whole spectrum of current research on the Constitution and its origins. In one sense, from the perspective of the Army and the Constitution, the two thematic "bookends" are Professor Higginbotham's masterful analysis of the commander of the Continental Army's contribution to constitutional thought and a paper by then Chief of Military History William H. Stofft that revisits the constitutional basis of civilian control over military power. Other subjects were as varied as the role of James Madison at the Constitutional Convention, Charles Beard's economic interpretation of the creation of the Constitution, the origins of American constitutional thought, and the Constitution and the militia.

In partial fulfillment of its mission to "ensure the complete and appropriate use of military historical experience relevant to professional issues of today and tomorrow," the U.S. Army Center of Military History is now publishing these lectures and papers in this volume. In doing so, the Center hopes that these studies will help soldiers better appreciate and understand the living document to which they have pledged their solemn oath. The Center is also making the volume available, through the Government Printing Office, to scholars and others interested in the Constitution and in is impact on military affairs.

As a last note, all but one of these pieces were prepared by their authors in discursive manuscript form. The one exception is Professor A. E. Dick Howard's "The Constitution: Today and Tomorrow," which is an edited transcription of his lecture. His remarks clearly have a different cadence from the preceding papers; in many respects they bring the collection together, insofar as he refers to so many of the key issues in our constitutional heritage. Consequently, his relatively informal lecture concludes the book, after the two supplemental papers. The volume was ably copy edited by Mrs. Rae T. Panella.

8 February 1990   JOHN W. ELSBERG

Contents

Acknowledgement: The frontispiece, George Washington at Princeton, by Charles Willson Peale, is from the U.S. Capitol Collection.

PAPERS
on
THE CONSTITUTION

George Washington's Contributions to American Constitutionalism

by

Don Higginbotham

The title of this essay may seem perplexing since we are not in the habit of associating military men with the establishment of enduring constitutional forms that provide for civilian governments and basic human rights. Certainly, in our own century the trend has been in a very different direction. I discovered, in looking for statistical information on this subject, some sobering figures. At that time, thirty-two of the fifty-one nations that existed in 1917 had subsequently known military takeovers, and so had fifteen of the twenty-eight states born between the end of World War I and 1955. The trend toward rule by the sword, either open or veiled, seems to have accelerated during the last three decades.

Americans of the Revolutionary generation were keenly aware of the dangers of militarism. Educated in the classical tradition, they knew that conquering armies of antiquity had turned upon their own governments and established despotic regimes. In Rome, the most frequently cited example, the military, lacking adequate civil control, had contributed to the demise of the republic.

But Americans had more recent examples in the case of their own mother country. After Charles I inflamed Englishmen by billeting troops in private homes and committing other infringements on ancient liberties, Parliament compelled the king in 1628 to sign the Petition of Right, containing provisions against martial law and arbitrary quartering. Parliament itself was threatened by the "New Model" army during the English civil war, and under Cromwell the nation suffered from military rule. The restoration of the Stuart monarchy in 1660 soon saw new complaints of military dangers as both Charles II and James II maintained substantial numbers of men under arms in peacetime. Consequently, the Restoration witnessed the birth of the classic English ideological opposition to militarism, which took the form not only of a suspicion of armies in general but especially of "standing armies": permanent establishments supplied by the public treasury in peace as well as war.[1]

If the Glorious Revolution of 1688 removed any martial threat from James II, and if Parliament guaranteed its jurisdiction in the military sphere by proclaiming in the Bill of Rights "That the raising or keeping of a standing army within the kingdom in time of peace, unless it be with the consent of parliament is against the law," should we then assume that the fear of armies in the Anglo-American world had become a dead issue? In fact, that was not the case for the English colonists (although the issue was largely dormant in Britain itself after the seventeenth century). The imperial wars with France of the following century brought extensive colonial contact with British armies, and much of that interaction was acrimonious, involving disputes over such matters as quartering, supplies, and enlistments. New civil-military controversies erupted in the years just before the American Revolution when redcoats were sent to Boston in 1768 and again in 1774 to enforce unpopular British measures.[2]

From all the above, we might conclude that a commanding general in the American Revolution would be viewed so suspiciously that he could hardly contribute substantially to the making of a great political charter. But it can be demonstrated that Washington contributed in two significant ways: first, by his behavior as Commander in Chief of the Continental Army; and, second, by his efforts both during and after the war in behalf of a firm American Union.

We can scarcely address these two achievements without initially noting experiences in his pre-Revolutionary background that enabled him later to transcend the traditional suspicion of military men and to speak with authority on broad questions of a political and constitutional nature. Those experiences were also crucial to his overcoming rather serious youthful frailties, which had clearly manifested themselves during his command of the Virginia forces during the French and Indian War.

Though displaying far greater ability as a provincial soldier than has usually been recognized, Washington had a tendency to blame others for obstacles not easily overcome in a frontier struggle marked by shortages of men and equipment, home-front apathy, and cumbersome governmental machinery. When Washington did not obtain satisfaction from Virginia's Governor Robert Dinwiddie, he circumvented his direct civilian superior by dashing off letters critical of the chief executive to other colonial leaders; and at times his behind-the-back barbs fell on legislators as well— "Chimney Corner Politicians," he called them. Washington would not be the last American military man to be provoked by the slowness and awkwardness of the democratic political process, even when those commanders acknowledged their commitment to civilian control. Nor would he be the last American commander to be encouraged to act in ways that bordered on defiance of constituted authority. For example, Richard Bland, a member of the House of Burgesses, assured Washington that "Generals and Commanders of Armies must be left to act as they find it most expedient for their Country's Interest" in times of crisis.[3]

How did Washington widen his horizons so as to appreciate civilian views and to recognize the restraints that retard the effectiveness of political bodies? The answer, in a nutshell, is that Washington himself moved from the commander's tent to the legislator's hall, first to the Virginia House of Burgesses in 1758 and then to the Revolutionary Continental Congress in 1774. During his decade and a half as a Virginia legislator, Washington learned that impulsive tendencies were counterproductive in a deliberative political forum; that the burgesses looked at domestic matters from a strikingly different angle of vision from that of a soldier. The same lessons held true in the Continental Congress, and perhaps even more so since the delegates at Philadelphia came from twelve, and eventually thirteen, colonies, men of diverse interests and backgrounds who were often suspicious and jealous of one another. Thus, in Williamsburg and Philadelphia, Washington received invaluable lessons for his role as Commander in Chief of the American army in the War of Independence, just as he became more sensitive to the nature of the Anglo-American heritage of civil control of the military, a heritage that Britain herself seemed to threaten during the dark days of 1774–1775.

Now we are in a position to understand Washington's first contribution to American constitutionalism. His behavior as

Commander in Chief demonstrated to his countrymen that armies and their commanding generals must not necessarily be feared and that it was possible to write into a national parchment provisions for permanent military forces that would remain under civilian control and that would be loyal to the ideals of the Republic. After he was unanimously elected "General and Commander in Chief of the army of the United Colonies" in June of 1775, Washington made a brief acceptance speech. He promised to "exert every power I possess" in behalf of the American cause, although he modestly questioned whether he was equal to the high station accorded him.[4]

Washington set out to take over his army, which, after Lexington, Concord, and Bunker Hill, was besieging the forces of British General Thomas Gage in Boston. Surely the Virginian realized that Massachusetts was probably the colony most sensitive to military intrusion, not only because of Gage's regiments but also because throughout the eighteenth-century imperial wars the Bay province had known the presence of redcoats. Besides, "for over half of the period between 1689 and 1775" Massachusetts had for military purposes "mustered and taxed its inhabitants to a degree unduplicated in any other British colony."[5]

The new Commander in Chief issued addresses to the legislative bodies of both New York and Massachusetts, assuring them that he had only reluctantly given up "the Enjoyments of domestic Life" for a station he had not solicited. He sought only for himself a part in restoring "Peace, Liberty and Safety." Here and elsewhere he often went to great pains to point out that there should be no gulf between the soldier and the civilian. "When we assumed the Soldier," he declared, "we did not lay aside the Citizen, & we shall most sincerely rejoice with you in that happy Hour when the establishment of American Liberty on the most firm & solid Foundations, shall enable us to return to our Private Stations in the bosom of a free, peaceful, & happy Country."[6]

His task was to make his army as well trained and professional as possible, so as to go head to head against his red-coated opponents, without making it seem like a European army. If he opposed such British army practices as permitting generals to have their own personal regiments as sinecures and allowing officers to buy and sell their commissions, he nonetheless had to request tactfully that the Continental Congress go against the grain of its Whig proclivities and enlist men in the service for more than a single year, which had been the initial practice of the army, a request that the Philadelphia lawmakers agreed to, albeit reluctantly.

When the British forces sailed away from Boston on March 17, 1776, Washington had more than a moral victory to boost his spirits. He had also, during his initial nine-month command in New England, demonstrated that his army had lived consistently with the principles of the Revolution. This is not to say that the future would witness no fears that the general might wish to become an American Caesar or that his army might desire to institute military rule. But such alarms represented the views of the few and not the many—the views of the most doctrinaire of the revolutionists, of whom every revolution has its share.

More typical of civilian attitudes toward Washington were those displayed by the Massachusetts Revolutionary government as Washington departed to do battle elsewhere against the legions of George III. The New Englanders stated that he had been "mild, yet strict" in his "government of the army," treating their sons and neighbors as citizen-soldiers rather than as European mercenaries. Even in the mdst of war and Revolution, he had adhered strictly "to the civil constitution of this colony." Washington, in response, acknowledged his concern for the Massachusetts constitution, as well as for "every Provincial institution," which would "ever form a part of my conduct."[7]

If he had built up a reservoir of trust and good will, he would need every bit of it in a war that was far from over, that dragged on for seven more agonizing years. And all the while, Washington was expected to respect the home front, to be the servant of Congress, and to be sensitive to the concerns of state and local officialdom. In retrospect, it may be that the most amazing thing about Washington's generalship was his ability to retain the respect of both the Army and the civilian population, since so often the two appeared to be in conflict because of the above-mentioned requirements imposed upon the Army's conduct and also because so often Congress and the civilian sector seemed to come up far short of meeting the Army's material needs.[8]

Prominent generals bluntly voiced their unhappiness. "There is a terrible falling off in public virtue since the commencement of the present contest," groused General Nathanael Greene in 1779. "The loss of Morals and the want of public spirit leaves" the Army "almost like a Rope of Sand." Congress, constituting the central government (such as it was), bore the brunt of the officers' complaints. Charles Lee, the third-ranking general in the Army, castigated the federal legislators for "having no military men in their body" and therefore "continually confounding themselves and everybody else in military matters."[9]

In such a tense atmosphere, punctuated by more battlefield defeats than victories and by stressful winter Army encampments at Valley Forge and Morristown, dire rumors seemed to threaten permanently civil-military relations. Three were perhaps most troubling.

First, there was the widely circulated, albeit erroneous, report in the winter of 1777–1778 that Congress, upset by Washington's defeats at Brandywine and Germantown, was about to replace the Commander in Chief with Horatio Gates, the victor over Burgoyne at Saratoga. Washington himself came to believe that a faction in and out of Congress sought his removal, an episode remembered as the Conway Cabal since General Thomas Conway was known to be critical of Washington and friendly to Gates. Though Washington lashed out at his alleged detractors, he remained respectful of Congress, and he assured the president of that body that he would always do its bidding. It might have been tempting to have implied to the lawmakers that the Army would stand behind him no matter what; but he never made even a veiled threat, nor did he encourage his zealously supportive officers to revile Congress for the reputed lack of faith in him on the part of some of its members.[10]

Second, there were rumors that some Americans wished to make Washington a king and that, given the corruptibility of human nature, the Virginian might become susceptible to schemes to replace George III with George I. John Adams, who complained of the "stupid veneration" accorded Washington, thanked heaven that Gates, not the Commander in Chief, had bested Burgoyne. Benjamin Rush, the distinguished Philadelphia physician, seems to have been the most fearful of all those Americans who recorded their sentiments on the subject. In 1777 Rush expressed the belief that Washington was keeping alive a respect for monarchy and that, urged on by myriad idolaters, he would soon assume an American throne.

Unquestionably, many of Washington's countrymen praised him in language reminiscent of kingship. We find countless references to "Washington the Great" in an age when European rulers bore such designations as Frederick the Great and Catherine the Great. Baroness Frederika Riedesel, wife of John Burgoyne's Brunswicker general, complained of having her sleep disturbed by Americans singing "God save great Washington: God damn the King."[11] But it should also be remembered that he was equally praised for his republican virtue, sacrifice, and dedication in behalf of a Revolution that proclaimed its rejection of Old World political ideas and institutions. In truth, Washington received plaudits that smacked both of monarchy and republicanism. He was the means by which multitudes of Americans "got monarchy out of their system without having to pay a fatal price for doing so, a rare instance of having one's cake and eating it too."[12]

Curiously enough, it seems that expressions of alarm like Rush's were much more prevalent early in the war than in the final years of the conflict. The explanation may be that Washington's dedication to civil supremacy and constitutional government had already been conclusively demonstrated on the anvil of adversity, and thus by the 1780s we encounter few references to the apprehensions of Adams and Rush.

Yet the only known direct attempt to encourage Washington to accept a crown occurred some months after Yorktown. It came to the Commander in Chief in the form of a seven-page essay from Colonel Lewis Nicola, an Irish-born Huguenot, who argued that the inefficiency of Congress and the shabby treatment of the Continental Army had "shown to all, but to military men in particular the weakness of republics." In the colonel's opinion, America needed a Constitution that put considerable power in the hands of a single individual. Since "Republican bigots" would condemn his proposal, it might be well to employ "some title apparently more moderate" than that of king, although "strong arguments" could be advanced for that title and—so he clearly implied—for bestowing it upon Washington.

It was "with a mixture of great surprise and astonishment" that Washington responded to Nicola, whose creed left the Commander in Chief with "painful sensations" that were truly unmatched "in the course of the War" He was "much at a loss to conceive what part of my conduct could have given encouragement to an address which . . . seems big with mischiefs that can befall my Country . . . you could not have found a person to whom your schemes are more disagreeable." While he did acknowledge that the Army had not always received its just desserts, he would work to obtain them, but only in what he called "a constitutional way." That Washington wanted proof of his having replied with unequivocal disdain to Nicola is evidenced by his securing the signatures of his two aides-de-camp on his file draft of the letter. It was the only instance during the war of his taking such a precaution.[13]

The third of the most troubling civil-military rumors also involved Washington and the army, but it was that the army and Washington might part company because the officers considered him too loyal to Congress and therefore unable to secure the army's interests. This concern surfaced in 1782–1783 as the war wound down and as the officers feared that they would be dismissed before Congress dealt with their unpaid salaries and requests for postwar compensation. There were rumblings that the Army, supported by public creditors and a cluster of politicians, would refuse to disband until it received justice from Congress and that a military coup was not an impossibility. There were intriguers in the Army at the time—their activities known today as the Newburgh Conspiracy—but their efforts to unite the officers in behalf of strong tactics failed. The response of General Henry Knox to these machinations might well have become something of a creed for the American army, as valid for our time as for his. "I consider the reputation of the American Army as one of the most immaculate things on earth," he declared; "we should even suffer wrongs and injuries to the utmost verge of toleration rather than sully it in the least degree."[14]

Washington himself, however, played the key role in deflating the plotters, who had circulated two inflammatory papers—the so-called Newburgh Addresses—at his cantonment on the Hudson. Appearing before the officers, he denounced the threats and pressure tactics, which, if successful, would have set a dangerous precedent for the intervention of the American military in the political and constitutional processes of the nation. In the midst of his firm but conciliatory remarks, in which he promised to do his utmost to see that Congress dealt fairly with the Army, the Commander in Chief hesitated and then pulled out his new spectacles and put them on. Many did not realize that his sight had become impaired. As he fumbled in adjusting his glasses, he intoned apologetically, "Gentlemen, you will permit me to put on my spectacles, for I have not only grown gray but almost blind in the service of my country." His efforts, including his sense of the dramatic at Newburgh, pushed both the Army and Congress toward a resolution of their differences.[15]

Washington was keenly aware that military tensions are inherent in free and open societies—for the precise reason that the military does not have a blank check in such societies; and he strove successfully to keep those tensions from getting out of control. He demonstrated that a professional army was not incompatible with civil liberty and constitutional government.

That was the symbolic meaning attached to Washington's appearance before Congress at the conclusion of the war to resign his commission as Commander in Chief, an event that was as emotional and dramatic as his Newburgh speech. Bowing to the lawmakers, "under whose orders I have so long acted," the general announced that "I have now the honor of offering my sincere Congratulations to Congress and of presenting myself before them to surrender into their hands the trust committed to me, and to claim the indulgence of retiring from the Service of my Country." "You have," responded President Thomas Mifflin, "conducted the great military contest with wisdom and fortitude invariably regarding the civil power and through all disasters and changes.[16]

* * * *

Even so, Washington's first great contribution to American constitutionalism had been made in the course of hardships that sprang in part from constitutional government itself: specifically, the limited authority that the states had bestowed upon Congress, which, in fact, existed at the will of the states as an extralegal body before the ratification of the first national constitution, the Articles of Confederation, in 1781. The Articles, however, only confirmed the limited authority that Congress had exercised previously. Indeed, throughout the war, observed the French commander at Yorktown, the Comte de Rochambeau, Washington had suffered from what the foreigner called "an untenable military constitution."[17]

And how did Washington feel about this untenable constitution? Actually, he was quite critical of it both during and after the struggle—to the point that he was the most vocal and persistent critic of the American constitutional form of government. We would be terribly concerned if his counterpart today—the Chairman of the Joint Chiefs of Staff—persistently advocated altering or replacing our present political fabric. We might recall the legendary man on horseback who has trampled upon constitutionalism throughout Latin American history. But Washington's criticisms brought him little if any censure, and the reasons are clear enough. He had sufficiently demonstrated his commitment to civil control for his countrymen to realize that he constituted no personal threat. He wished to see political change take place in a peaceful and legal manner. And he campaigned to increase the authority of his civil master, the Continental Congress, not to lessen its jurisdiction and influence. His efforts in behalf of a muscular central government began early in his tenure as Commander in Chief, for he realized that without it winning the war would be difficult if not impossible. He never wavered from that view, nor from his corollary opinion that the state governments were a major obstacle to Congress' management of the nation's affairs.

If, throughout American history, the balance of power in federal-state relations has ebbed and flowed with the political mood of every generation, the Revolution was an era in which power tilted heavily in favor of the states. That fact made George Washington unhappy, and this very persistent, determined man sought to do something about it. Had Thomas Paine not preempted the phrase, we might entitle Washington's statements on government "common sense," because he rarely resorted to abstract principles or historical analogies, although he was better read and more familiar with the intellectual climate of his age than has been recognized. He believed that both men and nations were governed by self-interest. (His "knowledge of human nature," he said, had been learned during the dark days of the French and Indian War.) Progress came when self-interest could be joined to a broader interest. "I do not mean to exclude altogether the Idea of Patriotism," he declared, "I know it exists, and I know it has done much in the present Contest. But I will venture to assert, that a great and lasting War can never be supported on this principle alone. It must be aided by a prospect of Interest or some reward. For a time, it may, of itself push Men to Action; to bear much, to encounter difficulties; but it will not endure unassisted by Interest."[18]

Unlike a Paine or a John Adams, Washington never encapsulated his political thought into a pamphlet or book but chose instead to publicize his views through his private correspondence, which in itself is one of the great literary treasures of the Revolution. No other commanding general in our history has left such a sizable collection of now-published papers—they number in the thousands and fill twenty-five volumes. They show unequivocally that the Virginian was the first and foremost Nationalist of his generation.

In fact, he thought about boosting congressional authority over America before the Congress itself acted meaningfully to do so. Congress in appointing Washington Commander in Chief had not informed him of what latitude he had in making decisions relating to strategy and policy, nor had it instructed him whether he should be subject to the orders of colony-state officials in the regions where his army served. During his formative nine-month period of command outside Boston, Washington deferred to Congress on significant and sometimes trivial questions, and in so doing he set a proper example for other generals in his army. When New England civilian leaders sought his services for a variety of activities, he politely but firmly indicated that he held his commission from Congress and was not responsible to any local or regional political body. Thus, he seems to have been as conscious of setting vital precedents in the opening rounds of the conflict as he was upon entering the presidency more than a decade later.[19]

To state leaders, Washington voiced his sentiments in favor of strong government at both the state and federal levels. "To form a new Government requires infinite care and unbounded attention," he warned in 1776 as nearly everywhere provincial congresses were beginning to craft state charters from which would come what Washington trusted would be energetic political machinery; "for if the foundation is badly laid," he continued, "the superstructure must be bad. A matter of such moment cannot be the Work of a day." In Washington's judgment, however, their superstructures were not "firmly established." Governors had scant authority to respond decisively in emergencies, and public pressures intimidated legislatures from voting taxes, supplies, and manpower required to advance the military undertaking against Britain.[20]

While Washington admitted the hazards of forging new political instruments in the midst of war and revolution, he nonethe-

less repeatedly expressed disappointment that the threat to
America's survival had not hardened the cement of union. After
Congress in 1780 turned increasingly to the states for carrying a
greater proportion of the military burden, those political
entities—or so it appeared to Washington—were at their worst.
"The contest among the different States *now*," he complained, "is
not which shall do the most for the common cause, but which
shall do the least." They were "so tardy in collecting the[ir]
Taxes," he fumed, "that the most trivial sum cannot be obtained
for the most pressing purposes."[21]

As Washington saw it, the political system of the United States
revealed two glaring weaknesses: "the inability of Congress and
the tardiness of the States" in carrying out their responsibilities.[22]
He was not optimistic that the fortunes of Congress would improve with the ratification of the Articles of Confederation in
early 1781 because that document created only a loose union or
confederacy. As had been true throughout the war, the states
retained to themselves all powers over taxation and commerce.
Although the Articles stipulated that Congress could make war
and peace, it could hardly do so effectively unless the states
complied with congressional requisitions for men, equipment,
and money—and the Articles did not specify coercive authority
for Congress if the states failed to respond to appeals for support.

Only because Washington was usually tactful and diplomatic,
and because he made every exertion to obey state laws wherever
he took his army, can we explain why the Commander in Chief
remained highly respected by state officials at the same time that
he found so much fault with their governments' performances.
"General Washington complains of us all," sighed Joseph Reed,
president of the Supreme Executive Council of Pennsylvania, in
June 1781. "Engrossed with military affairs, he has not the time
or opportunity to know the real state of the country, or the difficulties which environ men in civil life."[23] Reed's perspective is
understandable, but Washington, the former legislator himself,
both at the provincial and congressional levels, and engaged in a
voluminous correspondence with civilians and soldiers alike, was
not uninformed about the problems of the states, even though he
might have conveyed more sympathy for long-suffering executives like Reed.

By 1780 at least, a year before ratification of the Articles,
Washington was the most persistent and outspoken advocate of

constitutional reform in America, and he remained so until the Federal Convention of 1787. The approach of peace in 1783 did not deflect him from continuing his appeals to shore up the hand of Congress. He was a man who always took the long view of things; and he knew that the problem of political instability would remain to bedevil the American Confederacy in the postwar era. Accordingly, in June of 1783, with his retirement in sight, he penned his most eloquent and important state paper, a circular letter to the governors and citizens of the states, a document that may have been more significant in its impact on contemporaries than his now-famous Farewell Address; it was printed and re-printed in the following years and was considered timely reading in 1787 by advocates of the Federal Constitution.

In this 4,000-word testimonial, Washington emphasized that "an indissoluble union" could be established only if, among other things, three objectives were realized: an adequate peacetime military force; "a sacred regard for public justice," which meant obligations owed to both soldiers and civilian creditors; and a recognition of common interests and a dispensing with "local prejudices." He concluded with a ringing challenge: how would the American people end the period "of their political proba-tion"? Now was the time "to establish or ruin their national Char-acter forever." Would they seize this "favorable moment to give such atone to our Federal Government, as will enable it to answer the ends of its institution," or would this prove to "be the ill-fated moment for relaxing the powers of the Union. . . . For, according to the system of Policy the States shall adopt . . . they will stand or fall." The question "is yet to be decided, whether the Revolution must ultimately be considered as a blessing or a curse: a blessing or a curse, not to the present age alone, for with our fate will the destiny of unborn Millions be involved."[24]

In the short run, however, Washington's appeal fell largely on deaf ears, and that is hardly surprising. A forward glance at the whole spectrum of American history (to say nothing of some reflection on the human condition) indicates that people rarely display reforming energies at the end of a long and costly war. Even members of Congress who had shared Washington's desire to bolster the Union retired from the national legislature and turned their attention to other matters for a time, as was true of Alexander Hamilton of New York and James Madison of Virginia. In contrast, Washington's last words as retiring Commander in

Chief, offered as a toast to his long-time lawmaker-employers, were, "Competent powers to Congress for general purposes."[25]

As Washington predicted, without reform, conditions did deteriorate: to the extent that by 1786 he was fearful of three possible scenarios for the country—anarchy, regional confederacies, or monarchy. Because of the nation's military weakness and lack of international prestige, Britain continued to occupy forts on the frontier in violation of the treaty of peace. Congress was unable to bargain with Spain in order for western farmers to ship their produce down the Mississippi or to prevent the Barbary Pirates from molesting American shipping in the Mediterranean. The government could not threaten Britain with retaliatory tariffs in order to secure trading rights in the West Indies, a step that would have eased the postwar depression, which was felt with particular severity in western Massachusetts in the form of Shays' Rebellion. And all the while, the states quarreled among themselves, faced the prospect of debtor outbursts like that of the Shaysites, and, in seemingly unending ways, snubbed their noses at Congress, which at times could not conduct business for want of a quorum.[26]

While Washington had never developed his own blueprint for curing the ills of the Confederacy, the truth of the matter is that few if any Americans before 1786—except for Alexander Hamilton and an occasional pseudonymous essayist—had gone beyond amendments to the Articles designed to enable Congress a measure of control over commerce and the authority to carry out its implied powers in the war-and-treaty-making areas. But as early as 1781 Washington hinted at something beyond such war-inspired alterations in the American political fabric when he called for "changing the present system and adopting another more consonant with the spirit of the nation, and more capable of activity and energy in public measures." By 1783 he had joined a handful of Nationalists, including Hamilton and Henry Knox, in thinking that neither Congress nor the states might be capable of initiating any successful political engineering and therefore, as he expressed it, "wish[ed] to see . . . a Convention of the People."[27]

Whether Washington was so fed up with localism and provincialism that he wished to abolish the states may be doubted, if for no other reason than the fact that he was ever the political realist. (He did say, however, "that there is more wickedness than ignorance in the conduct of the States.") But by 1786 his exasperation palpably knew no bounds. That was so even before the meeting of the Annapolis Convention in August of that year to discuss the states' common commercial problems and before the outbreak of Shays' Rebellion. His own sentiments with regard to the "federal Government" had long been "well known," he reminded Henry Lee in April; both "publicly and privately have they been communicated without reserve." "We have probably had too good an opinion of human nature in forming our confederation," he exclaimed to New Yorker John Jay, who served as Secretary of Foreign Affairs for the Confederation. He agreed with Jay that the Annapolis Convention would accomplish little, and that proved to be the case when only five of the thirteen states were represented at the Maryland city. Washington and Jay saw eye to eye on the need for a more general convention to look at all the problems of the Confederation.[28]

By this time Washington was convinced that not only should federal power be increased but that in specific areas the wings of "the thirteen sovereign independent disunited States" should be clipped. "Persuaded I am," he asserted, "that the primary cause of all our disorders lies in the different State governments, and in the tenacity of that power, which pervades the whole of their systems." As he indicated to Jay, "I do not conceive we can exist long as a nation without having lodged some where a power which will pervade the whole Union in as energetic a manner, as the authority of the State Governments extends over the several States."[29]

Strong language indeed! Here was a man who was ready to go beyond a few amendments to the Articles of Confederation, and the same was true of Henry Knox, Hamilton, Jay, Madison, and certain other Nationalists in 1786 and 1787. The central government must be liberated from its dependence on the states. To Washington, dependence was a dirty word. He said as much in fighting for his economic freedom from low tobacco prices and British creditors in the 1760s. He was in the 1780s an independent man who had fought for an independent nation, but the successful outcome of the war had not brought political independence for the nation, only political independence for the states, which he once translated as the "*monster*" of state sovereignty. As the need for a truly sovereign United States—with all of its power derived from "*the People*" (in Jay's words)—became increasingly evident to greater numbers of thoughtful Americans, Washington exchanged letters with Knox, Jay, and Madison that reveal their mutual concerns and objectives, which included the calling of a national convention.[30]

Once the Continental Congress, acting on the recommendation of the Annapolis Convention, issued its call for what was to become the Federal Convention, Madison tried out ideas on Washington that would later become part of the influential Virginia Plan. Some of those ideas were similar to the ones that Knox and Jay had tested on Washington in recent months. Washington was so impressed by their commonalities that he abstracted and assembled the pertinent parts of their letters for future reference (which he subsequently docketed "Sentiments of Mr. Jay—Genl. Knox and Mr. Madison on a form of Government previous to the General Convention held at Philadelphia in May 1787"). All proposed fundamental changes in the architecture of government rather than continuing to tinker with the specifics of congressional-state relations, which had been the objective of efforts to amend the Articles of Confederation earlier in the 1780s—efforts which Washington had always felt dealt too narrowly with revenues for Congress and not sufficiently with giving energy and authority to the central government in a broader sense.[31]

Washington's response was affirmative. He, of all people, hardly needed to be persuaded that the federal government needed not only added congressional power but separate executive and judicial divisions as well. He had long admired the Massachusetts Constitution of 1780, the only state document up to that time that provided for three reasonably independent and vigorous branches of government. Like Knox, Jay, and Madison, he stood ready to scrap the Articles entirely in order to provide "radical cures" for the nation's political ills.[32]

But would the states bow to such bold political engineering, and should he accept the position of delegate to the Convention that had been extended by the Virginia legislature? On both questions, he blew hot and cold. Initially, he seemed convinced that the people were not yet ready for such strong medicine—they might need a few more Shays-style uprisings and other calamities. The people—the democracy, as he described them—must "feel" before they "see." He seemed unwilling to take part in a gathering that might accomplish nothing; and, as he reminded his numerous epistolary friends, he had already informed the Society of the Cincinnati, an organization of which he was President-General, that he could not attend its triennial meeting, which was to take place in Philadelphia at the same time as the convention. But when his correspondents convinced him that his presence was indispensable, he agreed to their wishes. Besides, as he admitted to several, his failure to do so might be interpreted as a lack of concern; and it might even be misconstrued to mean that he hoped for a failure in the City of Brotherly Love so that he might play a larger political role at a later time. Implicitly, he appears to have been saying that some would see him holding out for the prospect of an American crown![33]

If Washington's criticisms of the existing political system in America had finally paid off, helping build momentum for constitutional reform, his association with the Philadelphia gathering was more important than anything he said from that time on. His selection as a delegate by Virginia—the second state to pick its delegation—encouraged the other states to send their luminaries to the Pennsylvania capital. His unanimous election as President of the Convention only further attested to the significance of the occasion—by prearrangement he was to be nominated by the 81-year-old Benjamin Franklin, the second most respected man in America[34]—but it also meant that his eminence and sense of fairmindedness would help keep the deliberations on course. And that was the case, as was his determination to achieve success. He set the delegates an example by attending every session and by always appearing on time, and he encouraged them to behave in the same manner, as, for instance, when he appealed to Hamilton, who had departed for New York, to return to the Convention.[35]

It is not easy to pinpoint Washington's specific contributions to the contents of the Constitution. His natural reserve and his role as presiding officer explain why he rarely expressed his own views on substantive matters. But he did reveal his support for a strong executive in various ways.[36] Some scholars feel that so much power would not have been written into the presidency, which represented such a radical departure from the American political experience, had it not been a forgone conclusion that Washington would be the first occupant of that high station and would set judicious precedents in exercising its authority. Some months after the convention, Pierce Butler, a delegate from

South Carolina, said as much: he did not "believe" executive power "would have been so great had not many of the members cast their eyes towards General Washington as President; and shaped their Ideas of the Powers to be given to a President, by their opinions Virtue."[37] If the Antifederalist James Monroe may have exaggerated Washington's great influence on the subsequent ratification of the Constitution, he nonetheless was not wildly off the mark in writing Jefferson that "assured[ly] his influence carried this government."[38]

To Washington, the Constitution was far from perfect—both he and Madison, for example, would have stripped even more authority from the states and lodged it in the central government. As it was, however, they had taken certain internal matters away from the states that had hardly seemed possible a year or two earlier. No longer could the states exercise sole control over their militias and retain full authority to put down insurrections within their own borders. Nor could the states print paper money and abrogate lawful contracts. Shays' Rebellion and other acts of lawlessness in 1786 had enabled Washington and the other nationalists to undertake those measures at the state level. And they may have been more rewarding to Washington than to most of the nationalists since he had long seen the need for both increasing the power of the central government and restricting that of the states.

In any event, Washington was, on balance, immensely satisfied with the outcome of seventeen weeks of labor at the Pennsylvania State House; and, given his seemingly failing attempts over so long a time to convince his countrymen of the need to create a new superstructure, we can understand his saying that the result was "little short of a miracle."[39] And maybe we can add that he himself was something of a miracle worker. The old saw that Patrick Henry talked for the Revolution, Washington fought for the Revolution, and Jefferson thought for the Revolution would seem inadequate so far as Washington is concerned. He talked a good deal for the Revolution, and he did some thinking as well.

Notes

1. Lois G. Schwoerer, *"No Standing Armies": The Antiarmy Ideology in Seventeenth-Century England* (Baltimore, 1974).

2. Douglas E. Leach, *Roots of Conflict: British Armed Forces and Colonial Americans, 1677–1763* (Chapel Hill, N.C., 1986); John Shy, *Toward Lexington: The Role of the British Army in the Coming of the American Revolution* (Princeton, N.J., 1965).

3. W. W. Abbot et al., eds., *The Papers of George Washington: Colonial Series*, 4 vols to date. (Charlottesville, Va., 1983–), 4:83; 3:347, n. 3.

4. James T. Flexner, *George Washington*, 4 vols. (Boston, 1967–1972), vol. 2, ch. 2; Douglas S. Freeman, *George Washington*, 7 vols. (New York, 1948–1957), vol. 3, ch. 18; Address to the Continental Congress [June 16, 1775], in W. W. Abbot and Philander D. Chase, eds. *The Papers of George Washington: Revolutionary War Series*, 2 vols. to date (Charlottesville, Va., 1985–), 1:1.

5. William Pencak. *War, Politics, and Revolution in Provincial Massachusetts* (Boston, 1981), ch. 11.

6. Abbot and Chase, eds., *Papers of Washington: Revolutionary War Series*, 1, 41, 59–60.

7. Hezekiah Niles. *Principles and Acts of the Revolution in America* (Baltimore, 1823), 149; John C. Fitzpatrick, ed., *The Writings of George Washington from the Original Manuscript Sources, 1745–1799*, 39 vols. (Washington, D.C., 1931–1944), 4:441. See also Don Higginbotham, *George Washington and the American Military Tradition* (Athens, Ga., 1985), ch. 2.

8. Don Higginbotham, "Military Leadership in the American Revolution," in *Leadership in the American Revolution*, Library of Congress Symposia on the American Revolution 3 (Washington, D.C., 1974): 91–111, and *Washington and the American Military Tradition*, ch. 3.

9. Richard K. Showman et al., eds., *The Papers of Nathanael Greene*, 4 vols. to date (Chapel Hill, N.C. 1976) 3:223. *The Lee Papers* (New-York Historical Society, *Collections* (1871–1874), 2:186.

10. The first scholars to discredit effectively the theory of a well-organized plot to remove Washington were Bernhard Knollenberg, *Washington and the Revolution* (New York, 1940); Kenneth R. Rossman, *Thomas Mifflin and the Politics of the American Revolution* (Chapel Hill, N.C., 1952).

11. [Francois-Jean], Marquis de Chastellux, *Travels in North America in the Years 1780, 1781 and 1782*, trans. Howard C. Rice, Jr., 2 vols. (Chapel Hill, N.C., 1963), 1, 287.

12. Don Higginbotham, "Washington the Unifier: Nationalism in the American Revolutionary Era" (an unpublished essay), 6. My interpretation of Washington's symbolic importance, as the quotation suggests, is that his countrymen had more of an addiction to monarchy than they were usually willing to admit. A recent investigation of the American veneration of Washington is Barry Schwartz, *George Washington: The Making of An American Symbol* (New York, 1987).

13. Fitzpatrick, ed., *Writings of Washington*, 14:272–73, 273 n. 81; John C. Fitzpatrick, *George Washington Himself: A Common-Sense Biography Written from His Manuscripts* (Indianapolis, 1933), 418. Though Washington had no taste for

a throne, monarchical sentiment found expression in some quarters at the time of the Constitutional Convention and in the 1790s (Louise B. Dunbar, *A Study of "Monarchical" Tendencies in the United States from 1776 to 1801* (Urbana, Ill., 1922), chs. 4–5; Douglass Adair, *Fame and the Founding Fathers*, ed. Trevor Colbourn (New York, 1974), 116–23).

14. Knox's remark appears in Richard H. Kohn, *Eagle and Sword: The Federalists and the Creation of the Military Establishment in America, 1783–1801* (New York, 1975), 27, which contains the fullest account of the Newburgh Conspiracy (ch. 2), although some of the author's conclusions are not universally accepted.

15. There are slight variations in the accounts of Washington's speech to the officers. Flexner, *Washington*, 11:507; Freeman, *Washington*, 3:435; 435, n. 39.

16. Fitzpatrick, ed., *Writings of Washington*, 27:284–85. Mifflin quoted in Higginbotham, *Washington and the American Military Tradition*, 105 and generally ch. 3, in which Washington's relations with Congress receive extended analysis. Congressional documents bearing on Washington's resignation are in Boyd et al., eds., *Papers of Jefferson*, 6:402–14. For expressions outside Congress on Washington's devotion to civil supremacy and voluntarily laying down his sword, see John Todd White, "Standing Armies in Time of War: Republican Theory and Military Practice during the American Revolution," Ph.D. dissertation, George Washington University, 1978, 339–40.

17. Quoted in Lee Kennett, *The French Forces in America, 1780–1783* (Westport, Conn., 1977), 83.

18. Fitzpatrick, ed., *Writings of Washington*, 10:363–64; 11:284–86.

19. Another initial military appointee who came from the ranks of Congress was Philip Schuyler, who commanded the Northern Department. He too deferred to Congress but nonetheless had a difficult relationship with the lawmakers, partly at least owing to state jealousies and congressional politics (Don R. Gerlach, *Proud Patriot: Philip Schuyler and the War of Independence, 1775–1783* (Syracuse, N.Y., 1987); Jonathan G. Rossie, *The Politics of Command in the American Revolution* (New York, 1975).

20. Fitzpatrick, ed., *Writings of Washington*, 5:20; Margaret B. Macmillan, *The War Governors in the American Revolution* (New York, 1943).

21. Ibid., 25:289.

22. Ibid., 26:186.

23. William B. Reed, *The Life and Correspondence of Joseph Reed*, 2 vols. (Philadelphia, 1847), 2:358.

24. Fitzpatrick, ed., *Writings of Washington*, 26:483–96.

25. Quoted in Freeman, *Washington*, 5:474.

26. The best recent accounts of the deterioration of Congress and the overall ills of the nation in the 1780s are in Jack N. Rakove, *The Beginnings of National Politics: An Interpretive History of the Continental Congress* (New York, 1979); Richard B. Morris, *The Forging of the Union, 1781–1789* (New York, 1987).

27. Fitzpatrick, ed., *Writings of Washington*, 21:109, 110; 27:49.

28. Henry P. Johnston, ed., *The Correspondence and Public Papers of John Jay*, 4 vols. (New York, 1891), 3:186–87, 203–05; Fitzpatrick, ed., *Writings of Washington*, 28:401–03, 421–23, 430–32, 485–87, 502, quotations on 402, 502.

29. Ibid., 28:502, 503; 29:238.

30. Fitzpatrick, ed., *Writings of Washington*, 29:50, 52, 70–72, 113–16, 152, 163, 172–73, 175–77, 188–91, quotation on 176; Johnston, ed., *Correspondence of Jay*, 3:203–05, 226–29, quotation on 229; William T. Hutchins, Robert A. Rutland et al., eds., *The Papers of James Madison*, 14 vols. to date (Chicago, 1962), 9:155–56, 166–67, 199–200, 224–25, 285–86, 314–16, 382–87.

31. Washington had written to Hamilton on March 4, 1783 that "unless Con-

gress have powers competent to all *general* purposes . . . the distress we have encountered . . . and the blood we have spilt in the course of an Eight years war, will avail us nothing" (Harold C. Syrett et al., eds., *The Papers of Alexander Hamilton*, 28 vols. (New York, 1961–1987), 3:277–79.

32. Fitzpatrick, ed., *Writings of Washington*, 18:298; 19:123, 192.

33. Ibid., 29:152, 170–73, 175–77, 187–88, 189, 192, 193, 194, 198–99, 208–10.

34. According to Madison, Franklin's poor health confined him to his home the day the President of the Convention was to be chosen. Consequently, another Pennsylvania delegate, Robert Morris, nominated Washington, whose name was seconded by John Rutledge of South Carolina. Rutledge added, declared Madison, that "the presence of Genl Washington forbade any observations on the occasion which might otherwise be proper" (Max Farrand, ed., *The Records of the Federal Convention of 1787*, rev. ed., 4 vols. (New Haven, Ct., 1937), 1:3.

35. Fitzpatrick, ed., *Writings of Washington*, 29:245.

36. Farrand, *Records of the Federal Convention*, 1:97, 2:121, 587.

37. Ibid., 3:302.

38. Boyd et al., eds., *Papers of Jefferson*, 13:351–52.

39. Fitzpatrick, ed., *Writings of Washington*, 29:409.

Madison's Career Peak:
The Federal Convention of 1787

by

Robert A. Rutland

Before the Bicentennial year is over most Americans ought to know what the Shays' Rebellion was, and they probably will have heard Thomas Jefferson's judgment that "a little rebellion now and then is a good thing, & as necessary in the political world as storms in the physical." Jefferson made that remark in a commentary on the Shays uprising that he sent to James Madison in January 1787. The Federal Convention in Philadelphia was already in the planning stage. Madison himself had been the prime mover behind the convention, and when he read Jefferson's radical statement we wonder whether he was amused or horrified. We can suspect the former, for Madison knew Jefferson too well to take all of his older friend's remarks at their face value. Rebellions were not anathema to men of Madison's generation anyway. They had embarked on one in 1775.

We need to be reminded of these facts because the Federal Convention and the Constitution are going to be praised and extolled a thousand times in coming months, and much of this warranted acclaim will come from people who are now afraid of revolutions. Our Revolution, as the precursor of the French Revolution, set in motion a complete change in the relationship of men to their governments. Not until the events of 1917 did we become skittish about the word, and I fear we did so for the wrong reasons. If the Founding Fathers built as well as we believe they did, why should the powerful ideas of the American Revolution be eclipsed by those of the Russian? If we hold those truths of 1776 as self-evident, then there is no reason to think in 1987 that respect for life, and liberty, and the pursuit of happiness is not as vital a goal now as it was two centuries ago.

Certainly James Madison thought that the intellectual warfare he was engaged in from 1776 onward had implications for all mankind. Sustained by that confidence in the goals of the American Revolution, Madison moved with a steadfast purpose as he headed for Philadelphia in the spring of 1787. We are now aware that Madison was the key figure in planning that meeting, and his powerful role on the Convention floor and in the ratification process is ample reason for giving him the title (which by the way he disclaimed) of "Father of the Constitution."

How Madison earned that title is the point of my remarks. I hope that after my case has been made, your understanding of this man's integrity and singleness of purpose will be greatly enhanced. Surely few Americans have given more to their country, and yet in the twilight of his lifetime Madison faced financial hardships and in common with Presidents Jefferson and Monroe he was almost at the end of his financial tether when death came. Whatever the nation's gratitude, it never showed up in his bank balance.

Although it is too late to help Madison so that his last days might be spent without worry about the source of his next dollar, we can repay posthumously his rich gifts to this nation by recognizing that he belongs on a special roster reserved for the likes of Washington, Jefferson, Jackson, and Lincoln.

One thing these men all shared was their belief that America was different, and as one of them said, America was mankind's "last, best hope." They also were chronic worriers—the lot of them. In Madison's case, he was always worried about the future of the nation more than about his personal welfare. It was this perception of a national malaise and a fear about where it was leading that forced him to maneuver the Virginia legislature into calling for a national meeting in Annapolis in 1786 to consider ways and means of mending the feeble Articles of Confederation.

Unfortunately, that poorly attended meeting brought forth no solution to the nation's financial problems. But out of the ashes of the Annapolis gathering (incidentally, the state of Maryland did not send a delegation) Madison and Alexander Hamilton thought they saw purpose in a second call. From his post in the Continental Congress, Madison successfully argued that another attempt should be made, to coincide with the scheduled meeting in May of the Society of Cincinnati in Philadelphia. More than any other American, Madison was responsible for the call for the Federal

Convention of 1787.

Perhaps Madison may have reasoned that if the country was going to fall apart, the best people ought to be present at the final tumble. But that is doubtful. He was not frightened by the reports from Massachusetts of armed, embittered farmers chasing sheriffs and judges away from tax sales, but he knew that General Washington was. Here was an opportunity, created by the fuss over the Shays uprising, which Madison knew how to exploit. Working behind the scenes, Madison obtained action in the Virginia legislature promising a delegation would be sent to that Philadelphia meeting. The makeup of that delegation, Madison reasoned, would in large measure determine the success of the Convention. And upon the success of the Convention rested the answer to Washington's rhetorical question of 1783, when he asked if the Revolution had been a blessing or a curse? The answer would be a curse, if the expectations of 1776 were allowed to wither and die. The answer Washington wanted to hear, and which Madison devoted his life to achieving, was that a blessing had been given to mankind in the form of a government that bestowed liberty and self-government on the American people. Plainly, Washington was discouraged. In the fall of 1786, after he read accounts of the Massachusetts uprising, Washington told Henry Lee of his despondency. Lee had suggested that things would not be set straight until Washington intervened and used his influence.

> You talk, my good Sir, of employing influence to appease the present tumults in Massachusetts. I know not where that influence is to be found; and if attainable, that it would be a proper remedy for the disorders. Influence is no Government. Let us have one by which our lives, liberties and properties will be secured; or let us know the worst at once.[1]

As a frequent visitor at Mount Vernon, Madison understood Washington's frustration; with the Convention scheduled for May, Madison took the measure of that frustration and appealed to Washington to serve on the Virginia delegation. Frankly, Madison implied, some of the best men in the country would come if Washington agreed to attend. The bill passed in Richmond named Washington as the first delegate on a distinguished list (Patrick Henry was named but declined), and his acceptance was essential.

Washington tried to avoid a commitment. He had worked to bring about changes in the hereditary nature of the Society of Cincinnati and thought his presence in Philadelphia, when the Convention was meeting, would be most awkward. Washington felt some embarrassment was likely, and so he threw the decision back to Madison. "Silence may be deceptions, or considered as disrespectful," he observed. "The implication of both, or either, I wish to avoid." Madison nudged Washington without pushing him. Leave the door open by not declining at once, Madison advised, "in case the gathering clouds should become so dark and menacing as to supersede every consideration, but that of our national existence or safety."[2]

Faced with that kind of an assessment, Washington knew where his duty lay. Within weeks after he received that Christmas Eve letter from Madison, Washington began planning for his trip to Philadelphia. Once newspapers up and down the Atlantic seaboard printed the news that Washington would be in Philadelphia, the other state legislatures hurriedly appointed delegations until a total of fifty-five men were under orders to be in Philadelphia in mid-May.

And these men were the best the country could offer— Alexander Hamilton, John Dickinson, James Wilson, Roger Sherman, Benjamin Franklin, John Rutledge, Charles Pinckney, Elbridge Gerry—all with service in the Continental Congress and many of them signers of the Declaration of Independence. Considering the relative brevity of the final document, it is noteworthy that thirty-nine of the fifty-five were lawyers. Lawyer, merchant, farmer, or chief, they were not going to miss the opportunity to serve once again with the great man. Washington's name assured the caliber of the delegates, and his presence was made possible by Madison's powers of persuasion.

Once it was clear that the Philadelphia Convention was a certainty, Madison bestirred himself among his books. He searched through histories of ancient and modern confederacies looking for evidence that could be applied to the American situation. Why had some republics prospered and others failed? Did the size of a country relate to the efficiency of its political institutions? Madison's scan of history led him to a conclusion that struck at the prevailing theories of the French writer Montesquieu. Every delegate was familiar with the French author's treatise, *The Spirit of Laws,* which praised the British constitution for its mixture of legislative, judicial and executive powers. What jarred the Americans was Montesquieu's insistence that republican government could not work in a large geographic area. If Montesquieu was right, the American experiment was doomed from the start because of the country's enormous size.

Not content with looking at the Old World for examples, Madison also dissected the various state governments and the confederation in America. The impotence of the Confederation, Madison concluded, was its inability to collect requisitions and prevent the states from encroaching on its authority. Moreover, the Confederation had no control over commerce between states or with foreign powers, and it lacked any means of forcing a recalcitrant state from a gross violation of the Articles of Confederation. States were supposed to meet their requisitions to the national Treasury, but if they failed to do so, there was no way to coerce the offender into a proper mode of action. From his own experience in both the Virginia legislature and the Continental Congress, Madison knew that nearly every state had a small band of powerful men who were jealous of any national authority. They wanted low taxes, or no taxes, and they repeatedly sought the easy way out of their local financial woes by passing tax relief measures or paper-money bills, and when it came time to pay bills due to the national Treasury they were full of excuses. Indeed, at the end of 1786, seven of the thirteen states had enacted some kind of tax relief or paper-money law which postponed the final reckoning for fiscal responsibility. Overhanging all this was the old war debt consisting of promises to pay lenders as much as fifty million dollars spent to win the war against England.

Thus Madison's main thrust was at the states, not the Articles of Confederation, and he made it plain in his analysis that the great problem in the United States was "the deficiencies and derelictions of the state governments."[3] Armed with his scholarly outlines, Madison constructed a plan which addressed the diagnosis of American pitfalls. No copy of this outline in his hand exists, but we know what was on his mind because he and the other Virginia delegates who arrived in Philadelphia early in May 1787 began holding daily meetings while they awaited a quorum.

Imagine a table in a Philadelphia hostelry where Washington, Madison, George Wythe, Edmund Randolph, John Blair, Dr. James McClurg, and George Mason were seated. They went right to work. In a letter to his son, George Mason explained what the

Virginia delegation was up to:

> The Virginia deputies (who are all here) meet & confer together two or three hours, every day; in order to form a proper Correspondence of Sentiments: and for Form's Sake, to see what new Deputies are arrived, & to grow into some acquaintance with each other. . . . The most prevalent idea . . . seems to be a total alteration of the present federal System and substituting a great National Council, or Parliament, consisting of two Branches of the Legislature . . . and an Executive.

The Congress, Mason said, would be "founded upon the Principles of equal proportionate Representation, with full legislative Powers upon all the Objects of the Union." To curb the state governments, he added, the national Congress would have "the Power of a Negative upon all such Laws, as they shall judge contrary to the Interest of the federal Union."[4]

In short, this was the Virginia plan that emerged by May 25, 1787, and we readily perceive that it was structured to meet the alterations Madison's research proved vital if the Republic was to survive.

Naturally, the Virginia delegates thought of proportional representation, for no state chafed more under the Articles of Confederation than the Old Dominion. How ridiculous, they reasoned, that Rhode Island with 40,000 citizens held the same voting powers as Virginia with ten times as many people. The problem was exacerbated by the conduct of Rhode Island in the postwar period, when state laws were enacted to force depreciated paper money on creditors; and to add salt to the wound, Rhode Island delegates voted against any proposal to create a national tax program through a duty on imports. The last straw was Rhode Island's refusal to appoint delegates to the Philadelphia Convention. When Madison heard that, he threw up his hands in disgust. "Nothing can exceed the wickedness and folly which continue to reign there," he observed. "All sense of Character as well as of Right is obliterated. Paper money is still their idol, though it is debased to 8 for 1."[5]

With Rhode Island for their whipping boy, the Virginia delegates took Madison's ideas and drafted a report which Governor Edmund Randolph (the titular head of the group) carried into the Philadelphia Convention. On the first day of real business, May 29, Randolph rose to present their handiwork. Fifteen resolutions were offered, embodying the main outlines of a republic based on a two-house legislature, an executive, a national court system, and a specific injunction that the new Congress would have the power "to legislate in all cases to which the separate States are incompetent." The new body could also veto "all laws passed by the several States, contravening in the opinion of the National Legislature[,] the articles of Union."

Now the delegates had something to ponder, and in quick strokes they dropped any notion that they were going to try to revive the Articles of Confederation. By the end of their first week, the delegates had chosen Washington as their chairman, enjoined all members to secrecy of their proceedings (and thereby kept the newspapers from reporting their deliberations), and embarked on a venture to rewrite the national Constitution. This was heady stuff, and the delegates knew it. "The Eyes of the United States are turn'd upon this Assembly," George Mason noted, "& their Expectations raised to a very anxious degree. May God grant we may be able to gratify them, by establishing a wise & just government. . . . The revolt from Great Britain, & the formations of our new Governments at that time, were nothing compared to the great business now before us."

After the first few days of general accord, it became clear that the small-state delegations were on the defensive. The Virginia plan provision for proportional representation in both of the new Houses of Congress was the sticking point. There was general agreement on the way to admit new states into the Union, and no real argument over a court system operating at the national level, but the New Jersey, Connecticut, Delaware, and Maryland delegates were remiss when the matter of counting noses came under discussion. Madison and James Wilson of Pennsylvania were often on their feet, challenging the notion that each state deserved an equal voice in one of the legislative chambers. Early on, the idea that one branch might be based on population but that the upper body would have to have equal voices for all states was broached; and each time the large state delegates rejected the point as leading back to the old problems suffered under the confederation.

Madison's other great effort was to make the new Congress an arbiter over state laws, and hold the power to negative any state statute deemed contrary to the national interest. After over a month of wrangling, Madison saw his point was becoming unpopular. Instead of making a concession, he stubbornly persisted in arguing that if this power was dropped the state demagogues would continue to harass the national government. At the outset, Madison said this power was "absolutely necessary to a perfect system. . . . A negative was the mildest expedient that could be devised for preventing these mischiefs."[6] When a Delaware delegate insisted that this provision would simply allow the large states to "crush the small ones," Madison would not budge. "What would be the consequence to the small States of the dissolution of the Union wch. seemed likely to happen if no effectual substitute was made for the defective System existing?" Madison asked. Aware of the admiration so many delegates held for the British constitution, Madison made his argument stronger by claiming that the British empire was kept in "harmony & subordination" by the prerogative which allowed the crown to stifle "in the birth every Act of every part tending to discord or encroachment."[7] But Madison lost followers as the Convention veered in the direction of compromise, and by late July his plea for a negative on state laws gained no following.

We tend to forget that there was a time at the Federal Convention when the arguments were conducted with shouts and threats. Meanwhile, some delegates decided to return to their home states, often for personal business but sometimes out of anger. The New York delegation lost two of its three members when John Lansing, Jr., and Robert Yates decided that the Constitution being created was not what New York would either need or support. They packed up, leaving Alexander Hamilton as their lone representative. Before too long, Hamilton took a long leave of absence, but not before a long speech in which he praised the British constitution, admitted he was for more aristocratical principles than most Americans would support (such as senators appointed for life), and then caught a stage coach bound for Manhattan.

Meanwhile, New Hampshire delegates were mired down at home in red tape and afraid they could not afford to travel to Philadelphia. Eventually, they found the funds but did not arrive until late in July. Rhode Island, of course, ignored the whole affair as though it were being conducted on another planet.

Madison kept track of everything that was taking place, of course, for he had come to a far-reaching decision based on his earlier research. He determined that by using a kind of personal shorthand he could make notes on the speeches delivered each day and keep a journal of the Convention that would have enormous value as a historical document. With his strong sense of history, Madison realized that he was a witness to something new and unique in world history: a set of men meeting and deliberating in search of a method for governing a nation based on republican principles.

Madison also perceived that William Jackson, the man chosen to serve as secretary for the Convention, was not making records of debates but only of votes on resolutions. If he did not keep a full record, this vital moment in history might be lost, and though it placed a great strain on Madison (he later said that the business "almost killed him"), he never missed a single day of debates and thus left a complete record that remains our best source of knowledge for the proceedings from May 27 to September 17.

With considerable pain, we can assume, Madison recorded the debates which occurred in mid-July, when the great crisis on the matter of proportional representation threatened to wreck the Convention. Earlier, the New Jersey delegates proposed a counterresolution to amend the Virginia plan by creating an upper chamber of Congress where each state had an equal vote. Madison and other large-state delegates attacked the scheme as destructive of all their other gains, and reminded them that the Articles of Confederation had been mutilated during the drafting stage when similar tactics had been used in 1777.

Now, Madison warned, the same critical juncture had been reached in their deliberations. If the small states were not prepared to accept a government based on proportional representation, "they would probably accede to no Govt. which did not in great measure depend for its efficacy on their voluntary cooperation." In other words, a return to the chaos of the confederation years. Besides, Madison insisted, the small-state position was based on a false assumption. The real difference between the states was not mere size, but their geographic location:

> It seemed now to be pretty well understood that the real difference of interests lay, not between the large & small but between the N. & Southern States. The institution of slavery & its consequences formed the line of discrimination. There were 5 States on the South, 8 on the Northern side of this line. Should a proportional representation take place it was true, the

> North side would still outnumber the other: but not in
> the same degree, at this time; and every day would
> tend towards an equilibrium.

Here was Madison calling a spade a spade. But his argument
made no dent until the compromise first proposed by Connecticut was voted on, to base the lower house on population and the
upper only on state representation, and although Virginia opposed the concession it barely passed. From that moment on,
there was no other issue likely to bring the proceedings to a halt.

Madison was disappointed, but not crushed; and he had
learned a valuable lesson that he carried through the rest of a
long political career: in votes of great magnitude, some kind of
accommodation must be reached or the alternative is complete
failure. The ability to compromise became a fixture in American
politics, despite Madison's misgivings at the time. Eventually, as a
congressman and as President, he learned to accept half-victories.

At the time, Madison was momentarily fainthearted and he
was fearful that all their work to that moment had been for
naught. He kept his pessimism in check, and a few days later he
felt better. To Jefferson, his Virginia friend then serving as the
American minister in Paris, Madison simply reported that he was
under an injunction for secrecy so could not say anything about
the Convention's work. "I do not learn however that any discontent is expressed at the concealment," he told Jefferson, "and [I]
have little doubt that the people will be as ready to receive as we
shall be able to propose, a Government that will secure their
liberties & happiness."[8]

Once the compromise on representation was reached, the
delegates moved into higher gear and took on the tasks of defining the roles of Congress, setting forth a means of electing a
President, and reaching another settlement on the slavery issue.
There was no serious effort to try and end slavery, and after the
South Carolina delegates threatened to walk out, the issue smol-
dered until a solution of sorts was arranged. Slaves would not be
counted as citizens in assigning seats in Congress, except on a
ratio of three for five (50,000 slaves would be considered as
30,000 citizens in proportional representation). After 1808 no
slaves might be imported. These were crucial decisions, but the
delegates backed away from using the word "slave" and crusty old
George Mason would not let things fall into place that easily.
Allowing slave imports for another twenty years, Mason said,

would mean that Georgia and South Carolina (the only Southern states still allowing the importation of "persons of color") would monopolize the business. "Every master of slaves is born a petty tyrant," Mason said. "They bring the judgment of heaven on a Country. As nations cannot be rewarded or punished in the next world they must be in this."[9] Since Mason was one of the largest slaveholders at the Convention, his remarks were taken with a grain of salt. Mason grumbled more about the prohibition on slave-trading legislation, called the traffic in slaves "the most disgraceful thing in America," but then had to watch as the compromise was approved with the help of Northern votes.

Although the conducting of foreign affairs had been haphazard under the Articles of Confederation, the Convention delegates were leery of strictures on diplomacy. Lucky enough to have a Franklin, John Adams, and Jefferson for service abroad, the whole matter of handling diplomacy by a committee, as had been the case during the confederation, was now handed to the newly created executive. After long debate over how the President should be chosen, once they decided to use the imaginative electoral college their tendency was to leave unsettled matters still vague. The President was to be Commander in Chief, and thus ensure the supremacy of the military by a civilian, but diplomatic treaties could be made by the President with "the advice and consent" of the Senate. The power to appoint ambassadors, supreme court justices, and a whole host of other minor offices was vested in the President, but subject to Senate confirmation.

The Virginia plan contained a provision for a revisionary council that would work with the President "to examine every act of the National Legislature before it shall operate, & every act of a particular Legislature before a Negative thereon shall be final." This scheme lost support as the debates lengthened, until Madison was really its only defender. When even the right to negative unstable state laws was rejected, Madison believed he had failed on a fundamental issue. Sensing his disappointment, the delegates approved a clause which stated: "this Constitution . . . shall be the supreme law of the several States;" and ultimately it declared that the Constitution was "the Supreme Law of the Land." Clinton Rossiter says the delegates did this as a "consolation prize" for Madison; and in one sense, this sweeping clause offered a throttle on the states.[10] But the delegates went further with a long list of no-no's for the states. The states were prohibited from

coining money or making anything "but gold and silver Coin a
Tender in Payment of Debts" (so much for Rhode Islanders and
their paper money). Nor could states tax imports or exports, keep
troops in time of war, or make compacts with another state without the consent of Congress. These provisions made it likely that
Rhode Island would keep her distance, once the Convention sent
its handiwork forward, but that was the chance delegates were
willing to take. And a few, especially those from New England,
would have added: "good riddance."

Insofar as Madison was concerned, he was not worried about
the hasty manner in which the section on presidential selection
and power was drafted, since he believed that Congress would be
the dominant branch of the government. In his view, the branch
of government closest to the people should be predominant, and
he held this view as a basic tenet of republican doctrine. A second
overriding factor was the well-known assumption that Washington would be the first President. There seems to have been an
implicit feeling that Washington's performance in office would be
precedent-setting, and so the delegates assumed that the integrity of the first President would become not only a model for
future Presidents, but somehow would become an integral part of
the executive branch. Even so, they had a cautionary view when
reminded of historical precedents such as Charles I, and so they
accepted a section (partly from Mason, with an assist from Madison) defining treason and permitting the impeachment of the
President or any other civil officer for treachery, bribery, "or
other high Crimes and Misdemeanors."[11]

Madison was not alone in thinking that the President they had
created was to be subordinate to the Congress. Almost fifty years
after the Convention adjourned, the Frenchman Alexis de
Tocqueville studied their work and concluded:

> The Americans could not eliminate that tendency
> which leads legislative assemblies to take over the gov-
> ernment. . . . The President of the United States pos-
> sesses almost royal prerogatives which he has no occa-
> sion to use . . . [but] If the Union's existence were
> constantly menaced, and if its great interests were
> continually interwoven with those of other powerful
> nations, one would see the prestige of the executive
> growing, because of what was expected from it and of
> what it did.[12]

All this lay in the future, however, and a Committee of Detail
was appointed to begin applying some finishing touches to the
Constitution; Madison was passed over. How much difference he
might have made in filling in some of the cracks left from the
floor debate is only conjectural. The point is, his fellow delegates
were a bit in awe of the man. They could not let him be everywhere and do everything.

Proof of this judgment was left by the Georgian William
Pierce, whose notes included a summary of the abilities of his
fellow delegates. Pierce's assessment of Madison is one of the
fairest ever recorded:

> Mr. Madison is a character who has long been in pub-
> lic life; and what is very remarkable every Person
> seems to acknowledge his greatness. He blends to-
> gether the profound politician, with the Scholar. In
> the management of every great question he evidently
> took the lead in the Convention, and tho' he cannot be
> called an Orator, he is a most agreeable, eloquent, and
> convincing Speaker. From a spirit of industry and ap-
> plication which he possesses in a most eminent de-
> gree, he always comes forward the best informed Man
> of any point in debate. The affairs of the United
> States, he perhaps, has the most correct knowledge of,
> of any Man in the Union. He has been twice a Mem-
> ber of Congress, and was always thought one of the
> ablest Members that ever sat in that Council.[13]

Consider that Madison was thirty-six when these lines were written. No wonder Pierce ended his notes by saying of Madison: "He
is easy and unreserved among his acquaintance, and has a most
agreeable style of conversation."

The Committee of Detail was a businesslike body that got
down to specifics by taking the general resolutions and making
them into a list of explicit powers for Congress, and threw in a
catchall phrase that the newly created legislators would also have
the power to make "all laws" that were deemed "necessary and
proper." Its other great contribution was to set down all the
prohibitions on state governments, which skirted the struck-down
negative Madison had failed to carry by forbidding states to coin
money, issue bills of credit, make treaties, "keep troops or ships of
war in time of peace," and in general pulled the fangs out of the
Statehouse vipers that had enfeebled the old confederation. And,
to prevent the kind of impasse that had been ruinous under the

Articles of Confederation's unanimity rule, the Constitution was to become operative if ratified by a certain number of states (the exact number was still a blank space on August 6), but the implication was clear that the old unanimity rule was to be abandoned. Madison was, in a sense, the ghost at the committee table whose unseen presence was still felt and accommodated.

During the debates after the committee reported and before September 10 Madison was back in the thick of things, trying to curb the growing restlessness. When the quixotic John Francis Mercer of Maryland rose to denounce the emerging plan, Madison recorded the fact but knew something of the gentleman's personality and was probably not too distressed as Mercer stomped out and headed for home. Madison was among the delegates who moved to strengthen the President's hand, by requiring a three-fourths rather than two-thirds majority in each House to override an executive veto. But the only major problem as the delegates moved toward a final draft was something Madison could not have anticipated. When Randolph and Mason from his own delegation also revealed their misgivings and began to talk of the need for a second Convention or even a quickly drafted bill of rights, Madison lost his patience. Most of the delegates wanted to finish the business, not add to it, and Mason's pleas for a declaration of rights (which he assured them could be speedily whipped into shape) were rejected. With hindsight we know the rebuff of Mason's suggestion was to jeopardize all the good work of the preceding months. At the time, Madison and the majority thought Mason's surly demand was ill-timed and not worth a second thought.

In the final days of the Convention, Madison had some second thoughts himself. Although many curbs on state powers were evident, Madison still feared the motives of state politicians. To circumvent these rascals, the delegates provided that the emerging Constitution would go to special ratifying conventions, not to sitting state legislatures for their approval or rejection. Strategically, this was a brilliant move, made for obvious reasons. Already they could guess what the New York legislature might do, for had not two of their three delegates raced home in a huff? Would Rhode Island be any more reasonable? Special conventions would give friends of the Constitution a chance to bypass the naysayers in the statehouses. Instead of thirteen state ratifications, the delegates ultimately decided that three-fourths of the states would be sufficient to start the wheels of the new government rolling: Nine would be the magic number inserted in the committee's blank space. In specially called elections, the friends of the new government could exert their political strength by proposing candidates known to favor a stronger central government and then electing them. To smooth the way, a brilliantly worded letter of transmittal, signed by Washington, was to precede the Constitution. Clever Gouverneur Morris, who drafted the letter for the great man's signature, reasoned that readers would interpret it as conveying Washington's complete endorsement of the Constitution. And, generally speaking, that was the public's interpretation. The letter was worth its weight in gold, a million times over, to the Federalists.

Even with Washington's testimonial and Franklin's last-minute maneuver which made it appear that the Constitution was signed by everybody present (the words "by the Unanimous consent of the States present" overlooked the fact that Gerry, Mason, and Randolph refused to sign it), there was cause for anxiety. In weeks ahead it became clear that the ratifying process would require far more management than Madison or any other supporter of the Constitution thought necessary in mid-September 1787. On the other hand, when the finished document came from the Committee on Style (Madison was on that committee) and was signed on September 17 by thirty-nine delegates, even Madison himself reviewed their proceedings with self-congratulation and was inclined to say that their accomplishment bordered on the miraculous.

A clue to some of the difficulties soon came to the surface in New York. After the signing ceremonies, Madison hurried back to Manhattan to resume his place in the Continental Congress. There, opposition to the Constitution was evident when the question of relaying the finished document to the states for action was debated. From within his own state delegation, Madison found Richard Henry Lee anxious to block the process with crippling devices. Lee had been in touch with Mason, and was upset that no bill of rights had been appended to the document. He had more grave reservations, but Madison and nine other Convention delegates who were back in Congress defeated this threat, and on September 28 they formed a majority that sent the Constitution to the states for consideration by "a convention of delegates chosen in each state by the people thereof." There was no relaxation for Madison, but the man seemed to thrive on the business.

In private, however, Madison was worried. Madison was encouraged when he learned that some respected Virginians such as Edmund Pendleton were pleased with the Constitution, but in a long letter to Jefferson written on October 24 he vented his fears. The negative on state laws, he said, "was finally rejected by a bare majority" and "without such a check in the whole over the parts, our system involves the evil of imperia in imperio." Failure to have this power "seems to have been mortal to the ancient Confederacies, and to be the disease of the modern." Moreover, he thought a negative on states would have been useful in protecting individuals against an encroachment of their rights (and thus would have made talk of a bill of rights ridiculous). Because his pet scheme of a negative had been dropped, a state dominated by a majority united by a common interest or passion could oppress a minority in spite of all pleas for justice. Without the check which the Federal Convention had denied, Madison said, what good would it do to remind local politicians that honesty and fairness were the best policy? "They often proceed on the converse of the maxim: that whatever is politic is honest."[14]

In time, Jefferson assured Madison that his fears were probably unfounded, and that his judgment in rejecting a bill of rights had actually been a more serious failure. Events rushed forward to keep Madison from fretting for long.

The supporters of the Constitution had determined, in their informal meetings where tactics and strategy were discussed, that the faster the ratification process proceeded the better their chances would be. Once the Constitution was released, every newspaper in the country appears to have published it in toto (including the Washington testimonial letter), thus allowing readers in every state to determine for themselves its value. But to their dismay, Mason's hurried commentaries scribbled on a committee report had been rushed into print as a dissenting pamphlet. Labeled *George Mason's Objections*, the brief work began: "There is no Declaration of Rights." More Mason said, but his first sentence struck home.[15] Through the next ten months, try as they might, supporters of the Constitution (soon glorying in the name "Federalist") never were able to dispel the fears created by Mason's opening war cry. State politicians wary of the Constitution had other, and far more subtle, reasons to attack the new document; but they found the no-bill-of-rights charge a public rallying cry that threw Federalists on the defensive.

At first, Madison was not mindful of the hue and cry over an omitted bill of rights. Washington sent Madison a copy of Mason's pamphlet, and in reply Madison ignored the one which had the most public impact to dwell on matters of less substance. The quick chorus of dissent was the worrisome thing. "The newspapers here begin to teem with vehement & virulent calumniations of the proposed Govt.," Madison wrote Washington. "As they are chiefly borrowed from the Pennsylvania papers, you see them of course. The reports however from different quarters continue to be rather flattering."[16]

Madison was never one to whistle in the dark. His confidence was reinforced by the speedy ratification in Delaware, the rush to ratify in New Jersey, and rumors that Georgia was hurrying into the ratification column. The only bad news was that Pennsylvania Federalists, upset by the parliamentary tactics of a willful minority, had manhandled the recalcitrants in order to call a ratifying convention with unseemly dispatch. Philadelphia newspapers friendly to the opposition (now called "Antifederalists") cried "Foul." But the fact was that before Christmas day 1787 four states had ratified the Constitution. The battle lines indicated, however, that the crucial conventions lay ahead in Massachusetts, Virginia, and New York. A Union without those three states would be no Union at all, and everybody who had served at the Philadelphia Convention knew it.

As the instigator of the Federal Convention Madison possessed a certain amount of deference in Philadelphia. Now he was a member of the Continental Congress that would be replaced if the Constitution was ratified, and that gave him a franking privilege in the postal system. Night and day, from late October onward, Madison read every newspaper he could find, wrote potential delegates and erstwhile members of Congress in search of support, and urged friends to send him every scrap of news about ratification politics. In short, his desk was piled high with news both good and bad about the chances of gaining five more states by the summer of 1788. The wheels of government, meanwhile, were suspended. Except for the post office, the national government was doing virtually nothing; and the American emissaries abroad in London and Paris were keeping up appearances while borrowing money for their expenses from Dutch banking houses. No wonder Madison was worried.

Besides his volunteer duties as manager of a message center for the Federalists' ratification campaign, Madison had taken on more work in the precincts of his Manhattan boarding house. At Hamilton's urging, Madison agreed to help supply a steady flow of pro-Constitution essays to well-disposed newspapers in New York. Governor George Clinton had already fired his first attack on the Constitution, and it was clear that upstate New York would favor Clinton's Antifederalist position. An appeal to public opinion seemed the Federalists' only option. On Manhattan the dominant merchants were at odds with the governor, disgusted with his localism that harmed their commercial endeavors and prevented a profitable trade with international markets. These men had supported Hamilton earlier and were anxious to help him defy Clinton now.

The result of Hamilton's plan, abetted by Madison chiefly and slightly by John Jay, was the eighty-five essays published from October 1787 until May 1788 over the signature of "Publius." Known to history as *The Federalist*, these brilliant explanations of the Constitution and its theoretical base became a textbook for friends of the new document. Madison found time to write twenty-nine of the essays, keeping at the work until the spring of 1788, when he became involved in the preconvention shuffling for his home state's ratification struggle. Hamilton wrote the bulk of the papers, but Madison was an indispensable partner in the enterprise and particularly so when John Jay's illness in November 1787 forced him to the sidelines. Madison's first contribution, *Federalist* No. 10, would become the centerpiece of the whole series, and this essay is still used in classrooms and political discussions around the world.

The fame of *Federalist* No. 10 is owing to its bald statement of the facts: factions destroyed past republics but under the proposed Constitution the evils of factions will be mitigated by controlling them and channeling their energies into ends useful to society. At the Philadelphia Convention Madison had said the same thing, that the distribution of property was the main source of factions. Now he set his theory forth in black and white:

> Those who hold, and those who are without property, have ever formed distinct interests in society. Those who are creditors, and those who are debtors, fall under a like discrimination. A landed interest, a manufacturing interest, a mercantile interest, a monied in-

> terest, with many lesser interests, grow up of necessity
> in civilized nations and divide them into different
> classes, actuated by different sentiments and views.
> The regulation of these various and interfering inter-
> ests forms the principal task of modern legislation,
> and involves the spirit of party and faction in the
> necessary and ordinary operations of government.

So factions could be controlled, Madison hinted. Then he took on
the old idea of Montesquieu's that a republic could not survive in
a large country. Here Madison was at his most brilliant. Place a
diversity of factions in a large nation and they would be unable to
coordinate their selfish interests—the size of the country would
prevent their ready communication of special views and defeat
their strategy of unfair advantages.

Then, in *Federalist* No. 14, Madison became specific. "The
actual dimensions of the Union," Madison said, stretched the
United States along a mean distance of 973 miles north to south,
and 868 miles east to west. How could such an enormous country
be under the thumb of a single cabal? This reinforced his claim,
in the earlier essay, that elections in America would show that
unworthy candidates could not practice their "vicious arts" over a
large district. Instead, "the suffrages of the people being more
free, will be more likely to center on men who possess the most
attractive merit, and the most diffusive and established charac-
ters." Thus Madison stood Montesquieu's claim in the corner,
asserting that the diverse interests of the whole country would
combine, like the stakes and ropes that hold up a huge tent, to
provide the tension necessary for the success of the whole operation. In the two hundred years since Madison wrote, no other
American has come up with a more imaginative explanation for
what makes the Constitution "tick."

Besides writing for the New York newspapers (which meant
the essays were widely borrowed and reprinted), Madison
watched the goings-on in Boston. Early reports that the Antifederalists would be in command numerically proved true. Patrick Henry had managed the Virginia legislature's bill for a ratifying convention, setting the date for June in the hopes of
coordinating dissent with the New York gathering. Not to worry,
Madison insisted. To bolster Federalists in Boston, Madison assured Rufus King that despite Henry the situation in Virginia
looked good. "If nine States should precede it seems now to be

admitted on all hands that Virga. will accede," he wrote.[17] "Every post confirms the opinion that the Constn. is regaining its lost ground. It is impossible to express how much depends on the result of the deliberations of your Body."

The Antifederalists in Boston were numerous but essentially leaderless, and after Samuel Adams made a pitiful spectacle the Convention swallowed a dose of "recommendatory amendments" that made a case for a bill of rights *after* the new government was in operation. This sugar-coated pill went down by a 187–168 vote. In a rejoicing mood, Madison wrote Washington that the "amendments are a blemish . . . in the least Offensive form." Moreover, Madison told Washington, New Hampshire was holding its convention at that moment and the prospects were "that the issue there will add a *seventh* pillar." This report proved premature, for unexpected Antifederalist strength forced a postponement until June.

Meanwhile, Rhode Island legislators acknowledged the Constitution by calling for a public vote instead of a ratifying convention. Fearing the inevitable, Providence merchants boycotted the voting and the Antifederalist triumph was complete, as the Constitution was defeated in the only state where citizens voted directly in their town meetings, 2,708 to 237.[18]

Warned by his neighbors that Henry was trying to wreck the ratification process in Virginia, Madison left his command post in New York and hustled back to Orange County as a candidate for the Richmond convention. Madison looked elsewhere for the ninth pillar, after better news came from South Carolina. "Rhode Island have in fact rejected the constitution," a friend in Congress wrote, "so that only eight states can have adopted the system before the Session of Virginia. We all much rejoiced to hear of your election, especially as your being present, we are told, was absolutely necessary to counter-act some unwarrantable proceedings."[19]

What Madison heard was that Henry, in league with George Mason, was trying to make a package of amendments, including a bill of rights, as a *prior* condition for ratification. No ironclad provision to add these amendments, Henry insisted, meant no ratification. Election returns from the various counties indicated the friends and opponents of the Constitution were about evenly matched; some insiders thought the delegates sent from Kentucky would swing the balance and Madison sought to assure them (as Kentuckians talked of statehood) the Constitution was in their best interests.

A minor bombshell was dropped, after the Richmond convention opened on June 2, with Governor Randolph's desertion of Henry and Mason. Flabbergasted, Mason called Randolph a traitor and hoped to regroup by insisting on a long and drawn out, clause-by-clause debate. Madison gleefully accepted the challenge, thinking he would gain more time to work on the uncommitted delegates; and the Antifederalist's strategy backfired when Henry rambled all over the constitutional terrain in speeches that seemed great but proved to be unconvincing. John Marshall, who was there as a Federalist, recalled that Madison's clear logic was more than Henry's equal. Mason, once so confident that New York Antifederalists would cooperate by agreeing on an identical set of conditional amendments, was ineffective in his rhetorical flights of if's and but's. From New York, Madison was informed by Hamilton that some kind of New York–Virginia scheme was the Antifederalists' strategy. "We have conjectured for some days that the policy is to spin out the [Richmond] Session in order to receive overtures from your Convention," Madison wrote Hamilton, "or if that cannot be[,] to weary the members into an adjournment without making any decision."[20]

Day by day, Madison used his eloquence rather than his lungs to convince the Virginians of the crisis they faced. He had not come down the trail from Annapolis to Philadelphia and now to Richmond in order to fail. And he did not fail, as the final vote on June 25 revealed that eighty-nine Federalists had prevailed over seventy-nine Antifederalists to pass an unconditional ratification. Unbeknownst was the New Hampshire ratification a few days earlier. Thus Virginia was the tenth state to ratify, and after some graceless backing and filling the New York convention voted to become the eleventh approving state.

Madison's job was not finished, of course. His battle with Patrick Henry continued, forcing him to run against his good friend James Monroe for a seat in the newly created House of Representatives. The campaign involved promises to the Baptists in his district who had heard rumors that Madison was not in favor of a bill of rights or specific provisions to guarantee religious freedom under the Constitution. To kill these rumors Madison wrote a Baptist minister in Culpeper County admitting that he had not seen the need for a bill of rights as a condition for ratification. "Circumstances are now changed," Madison wrote.

> The Constitution is established on the ratifications of
> eleven States and a very great majority of the people of
> America; and amendments, if pursued with a proper
> moderation and in a proper mode, will be not only
> safe, but may serve the double purpose of satisfying
> the minds of well meaning opponents, and of provid-
> ing additional guards in favor of liberty. Under this
> change of circumstances, it is my sincere opinion that
> the Constitution ought to be revised.

The rights which ought to be added, he said, included "all the
essential rights, particularly the rights of Conscience in the fullest
latitude, the freedom of the press, trials by jury, security against
general warrants, &c."[21] That did the trick, for Madison went on
to defeat Monroe handily.

Once the new Congress was in operation, Madison quickly
became a kind of floor leader in the House of Representatives.
The main business was to pass legislation for tax revenues and the
regulation of commerce, but Madison was not backward in re-
minding his colleagues of the promised bill of rights. During the
summer of 1789 he bullied the House into appointing a committee to consider the sixteen suggested amendments he prepared
after studying reports from all the ratifying conventions. Widely
publicized, Madison's proposals forced the recalcitrant states of
North Carolina and Rhode Island to rethink their status outside
the Union. Pared down, twelve proposed amendments went to
the states for ratification. Ten survived, to become the Bill of
Rights. The impact of the delivered promise was tremendous,
and soon a full Union of thirteen states was also a reality.

Madison did not rest. He eventually broke with Hamilton over
the direction of American political policy and formed an alliance
with Jefferson that led to the creation of a new political party. But
on December 15, 1791, when the Bill of Rights was formally
ratified, Madison's credentials were already of the highest order.
He had done more than any other American to build the new
ship of state, he had guided her into a safe harbor, and he
believed that her rigging and timbers were sound enough for the
storms ahead. Madison was both the master builder and the pilot.
The Union was saved, and the twin goals of the Revolution—
liberty and self-government—were preserved for posterity. For
the time, Madison stopped worrying.

Notes

1. John C. Fitzpatrick, ed., *The Writings of George Washington*, 39 vols. (Washington, 1931–1944), 29:30.
2. William T. Hutchinson et al, eds., *The Papers of James Madison*, 17 vols to date (Chicago and Charlottesville, Va., 1962–), 9:216, 224.
3. Ibid., 9:346.
4. Robert A. Rutland, ed., *The Papers of George Mason*, 3 vols. (Chapel Hill, N.C., 1970), 3:880.
5. Hutchinson, *Madison Papers*, 9:362.
6. Ibid., 10:41.
7. Ibid., 10:103.
8. Ibid., 10:105.
9. Rutland, *Mason Papers*, 3:966.
10. Clinton Rossiter, *1787: The Grand Convention* (New York, 1966), 197.
11. Max Farrand, ed., *The Records of the Federal Convention*, 4 vols. (New Haven, Ct., 1911–1937), 2:349.
12. Alexis de Tocqueville, *Democracy in America*, ed. by J.P. Mayer and Max Lerner (New York, 1966), 110, 114.
13. Farrand, *Records of the Federal Convention*, 3:94–95.
14. Hutchinson, *Madison Papers*, 10:213.
15. Rutland, *Mason Papers*, 3:991.
16. Hutchinson, *Madison Papers*, 10:197.
17. Ibid., 10:409.
18. Forrest McDonald, *We the People: The Economic Origins of the Constitution* (Chicago, 1958), 322.
19. Hutchinson, *Madison Papers*, 11:11.
20. Ibid., 11:144.
21. Ibid., 11:404–05.

Charles Beard Revisited: The Revolutionary Debt and the Federal Constitution

by

Richard Buel, Jr.

I

In 1913, Charles A. Beard published the most controversial book ever written in American history, *An Economic Interpretation of the Constitution of the United States*. In it, he argued that the "movement for the Constitution . . . was originated and carried through . . . by a small and active group of men immediately interested through their personal possessions in the outcome of their labors."[1] Specifically, he was referring to the holders of the continent's Revolutionary debt. Congress had begun to consolidate this debt in 1782, but had no authority to pay it except by the ineffectual means of requisitioning the states, with the result that it had quickly depreciated to a point where it was of interest principally to speculators.

Beard argued that ownership of this form of personal property drove the Framers of the Constitution to seek a new government with sufficient powers to give it a value that it had not hitherto enjoyed. He stressed the antipopulist mode of their proceedings, noting that the majority of the people, who held real as opposed to personal property, had not been directly consulted by those who called the Philadelphia Convention, and that "probably not more than one-sixth of the adult males" qualified to vote had in fact voted to ratify the Constitution. Thus he concluded: "The Constitution was essentially an economic document based upon the concept that the fundamental private rights of property are anterior to government and morally beyond the reach of popular majorities." "The Constitution was not created by 'the whole people' nor by 'the states', but by 'a consolidated group whose interests knew no state boundaries and were truly national in their scope.'"

Beard's book met with a stormy reception. The Marion *Ohio Star*, Warren G. Harding's paper, ran a headline that proclaimed: "SCAVENGERS, HYENA-LIKE, DESECRATE THE GRAVES OF THE DEAD PATRIOTS WE REVERE."[2] William Howard Taft, though less extreme in his response, went out of his way to condemn the book in an address to more than a thousand lawyers and politicians in New York.[3] Though the book received some favorable notices as well,[4] many Americans, still only fifty years removed from the rending conflicts of the Civil War, recoiled from the desanctifying of what they had come to regard as an almost holy symbol of national unity.[5]

By contrast, the academic reception of the book was more skeptical than passionate. Though the *Economic Interpretation* invited commentary from political scientists, economists, and sociologists as well as historians, Beard's assumption of cold economic rationalism on the part of the Framers made his whole argument appear regressive to those social scientists who were bent on repudiating the "myth of the Economic Man."[6] And those who took the book on its own terms found other problems in it. Some observed that by Beard's own account the leading proponents of the new government in the Constitutional Convention held far fewer public securities than their opponents.[7] The distinguished constitutional scholar Edwin S. Corwin questioned the soundness of an argument that inferred what securities were held in 1787 from records made in 1790 or later.[8] Still others noted that the preponderant influence of the agrarian interest in all the states made it unlikely that their legislatures would have authorized the ratifying conventions, or that these conventions would ever have acquiesced in the Constitution, had they understood the controversy in Beard's terms.[9]

As so often happens with such an original and provocative book, it quickly faded from public sight. World War I engrossed popular attention, and though the thesis of the *Economic Interpretation* found its way into several influential texts during the 1920s, the academic world as a whole pursued its own peculiar priorities, which did not include further debate of Beard's findings. Not until 1935 on the eve of the Sesquicentennial of the

Constitution was the book finally reissued with a new Introduction. Once again, pressing matters intervened, but this time they paved the way for acceptance rather than rejection. The Great Depression of 1929 ruptured Americans' sense of continuity with their past and made them more receptive to Beard's conclusions.[10] Something had gone so badly wrong with the structure of American life that the myth of a sacred foundation no longer seemed worth preserving. Moreover, at a time when nothing seemed to be working, Americans were more inclined to admire the skill with which the Framers had pursued their political objectives than to condemn the possibility that they were interested parties. During the nineteen thirties, Beard's economic interpretation of the Constitution rapidly became the new orthodoxy of the so-called Progressive School of historians, particularly in college-level texts.[11]

Like most historical orthodoxies, its day was short, a casualty of World War II and its aftermath. Beard himself played an important part in the change with a series of dramatized conversations, entitled *The Republic*, recorded in 1943. Against the background of fascism and militarism, he was now prepared to attach more significance to the Framers' success in establishing constitutional government than to any personal interests they may have served in doing so.[12] In the immediate postwar period, several scholars followed Beard's revisionist lead by challenging various aspects of the notion that the Constitution had arrayed the interests of the few against the democratic aspirations of the populace, thus striking at the very core of the Progressive School's interpretation.[13] But it was not until the late fifties that Beard himself became the focus of attack. Then in quick succession Robert E. Brown's *Charles Beard and the Constitution* and Forrest McDonald's *We the People* sought to refute Beard's *Economic Interpretation*, Brown through a point-by-point rebuttal of Beard's argument, McDonald through a systematic examination of the economic interests of both the Framers and their opponents in the constitutional and the ratifying conventions.[14]

Of the two books, McDonald's has been the most influential because of its success in turning Beard's own method against his argument. McDonald refused to leap to the conclusion that holders of federal securities were only interested in that form of property. He sought instead to ascertain what other kinds of property they held, which forms of property constituted the larger portion of their total wealth, and how they expected to use that property. If, for instance, one had made a contract to buy public lands for public securities at a depreciated rate, one would have no interest in having these securities appreciate in value.[15] Only after determining what the delegates' principal interests really were did he ask if their behavior in the Convention could be explained by reference to them. And he found that, though a majority held public securities, their principal interests were too varied to make them into a coherent group; that the five largest security holders—in his phrase, an "all-star team"—refused to sign the Constitution;[16] and that there was no connection between the way a delegate voted on specific provisions of the document and his personal economic interests.[17] McDonald found a similar lack of correlation between possession of public securities and advocacy of the Constitution in most of the ratifying conventions.[18] Therefore, he concluded, the facts did not warrant Beard's claim that the ownership of the public debt provided the dynamic force behind the drafting and ratification of the Constitution.[19]

Yet McDonald did not put an end to the fascination of American historians with the Beard thesis. In the late 1980s, Richard Hofstadter, leading spokesman of the so-called Consensus School, published his study of *The Progressive Historians*, more than a third of its text devoted to an examination of Beard's career. It is perhaps worth asking why Hofstadter chose to focus his discussion on Beard's *An Economic Interpretation*, which had stressed how seriously Americans had been divided at the birth of the nation, where Hofstadter's own interest lay in identifying what is was that united Americans. The answer, I think, is that if Hofstadter could bring Beard within the mainstream traditions of American historiography, he would have succeeded in domesticating one of the most stridently critical voices in the nation's past. In this attempt, Hofstadter pursued his classic strategy of identifying an ambiguity in his subject's thought.[20] In Beard's case, this was the tug between the muckraking rebel, eager to expose the sordid reality that lay behind noble pretensions, and the honest admirer of the practical genius displayed by those who knew what they wanted and got it in spite of formidable obstacles.[21] For Hofstadter, Beard was right to introduce a note of realism into our understanding of the Constitution by insisting on the connection that exists between ideas and interests. He believed that this realism was necessary if we were to understand the emergence of the modern American state, which had its beginnings in the Revolution and the Constitution.[22] Thus he saw Beard as an essential contributor to emergence of our present national consciousness.

At the same time Hofstadter saw the limitations of Beard's approach. "[E]xcept for Beard's concern with the undeniably important Revolutionary debt," he wrote, "it is the persistent impact of the *Revolutionary experience* that one misses most in his account of the Constitution. . . . In his concern with the conflicting material interests left in the wake of the Revolution, he loses touch with the moving force of Revolutionary commitment." Hofstadter saw Beard's focus on the debt as a red herring,[23] but, in fact, neither Beard nor Hofstadter understood the debt, nor why people were interested in it at the time. The shortcomings of Beard's analysis proceeded from his rigid commitment to a narrow conception of "interest" which he hoped would give his conclusions a scientific rigor. If we reconstruct the reasons why even those who did not own the debt were interested in it, however, we shall see that Beard was, contrary to Hofstadter, looking straight at the clearest possible evidence of "the persistent impact of the *Revolutionary experience*," without realizing it.

II

Revolutionary ideology celebrated virtue, the willingness of individuals to sacrifice private interest to public good, and condemned corruption, or actions dictated by selfish, mercenary motives.[24] We might conclude, then, that the revolutionaries viewed the marketplace with suspicion.[25] Yet when we look at their actual behavior as they mobilized for the Revolutionary War, we are struck by their reliance on it. The first call for troops by the New England states offered good wages and met with an enthusiastic response. All subsequent attempts to raise men that I know of tried to offer an exchange of equivalents to the volunteers. As the war dragged on, Congress and the states gradually lost the power to offer creditable monetary incentives. But they strove to offer something, whether it was exemption from suits for debt, or relief from taxes. In addition, local communities tried to put up a purse themselves in order to make good the state's shortfall, at first voluntarily, and later under legislative compulsion. The act of drafting men was never used except as a last, desperate alternative, and even then every subsequent means was employed to induce those who had been drafted to become volunteers.[26]

The emphasis on volunteerism was not only congruent with ideas of republican virtue, but also made good military sense. Men pressed into service were less likely to show fight in battle, and more likely to desert. A man who enlisted in return for an offer of money, however, might still qualify as a volunteer in spirit. The marketplace also helped to establish a rough form of equality. Though it was impossible to equalize the misadventures that men would experience in battle, society could recognize that those who fought risked more than those who stayed at home. At the same time, those who fed and supplied the Army also had a claim on society. The bills of credit offered to soldier, farmer, and merchant alike in exchange for their resources or for the service they performed represented an attempt to equalize the burdens they assumed in supporting the cause, a token of the debt owed by the Republic to all those who were helping to secure its existence.

The marketplace and public credit, then, were recognized from the start as crucial to the success of the Revolution. That recognition, however, became a burden when, in the later years of the war, neither Congress nor the states could maintain the value of their bills of credit. Typically, the depreciation has been attributed to the excessive supply of bills.[27] In actuality, that was only part of the story. In relation to what was the supply of bills excessive? Both state and congressional bills held their value reasonably well through the first year of hostilities, and only began to depreciate after the defeats on Long Island and at New York raised doubts as to whether the Revolution would succeed. Thereafter, nothing could stop the depreciation, not even attempts to call in all the outstanding issues. Of course, these attempts were never wholly successful; nevertheless one might have expected that the policy of strenuous taxation pursued by Congress and the states after 1778 to have at the very least stabilized the value of the money.

That it did not had to do with certain structural problems in the American economy. Several anomalies in the long-term process of depreciation provide a clue to what these were. The one brief rise in the value of Continental money took place between April and June 1778, just after news arrived of the Franco-American Alliance, while some of the sharpest declines in value coincided with the failure of joint operations in 1778 and 1779.[28] These facts suggest that the Alliance had come to be regarded by Americans as the key not only to military victory but to economic health as well. The two, of course, were linked. A long war threatened to bankrupt the nation by saddling it with a debt it would never be able to pay. On the other hand a quick victory, or short of that, the resumption of opportunities, hitherto severely restricted by British naval supremacy, to exchange domestic surpluses for foreign imports, was needed if the domestic production of surpluses was to remain at anything like their prewar level.[29] The very process of this exchange created a firmer demand for the money than taxation was likely to,[30] because, once taxation became truly burdensome, there was little that could be done to stop people defaulting on their obligations. In the absence of an effectively centralized state, individuals charged with enforcing tax laws in their own localities were vulnerable to hostile pressures, pressures that could take many unpleasant forms including violence to persons.[31] The demand for money in trade, on the other hand, depended on the spontaneous operations of the marketplace rather than on coercion.

Unfortunately, the Franco-American Alliance, in its immediate effect, served only to bankrupt Congress and lock the continent into a war of attrition from which it could not escape on its own.[32] After 1778 the Revolutionary enterprise became mired in apparently hopeless difficulties. Nevertheless, France eventually produced the long-awaited deliverance. In the spring of 1780, aware that the authority of Congress was extremely precarious, the French government dispatched an expeditionary force to America. It was too weak to accomplish anything militarily, but it had to be fed and paid, and both these requirements introduced into the American economy much-needed remittances in the form of bills of exchange on France.[33] This development, along with French operations in the Caribbean, permitted the renewal of American overseas commerce, which in turn revived the incentives to expand domestic production. Now that there was something worthwhile to receive in exchange for one's goods, Americans once again began producing surpluses, which meant that they had the necessary provisions to support joint operations.

Then, in the following campaign, France gave them the added benefit of large direct subsidies, and, at the end of the summer, established naval superiority in the Chesapeake long enough to force the capitulation of Cornwallis. This blow broke the British will to fight on and paved the way for the negotiation of a peace. But victory was not a triumph for the Revolutionaries. Though there was much rejoicing at the news, the leadership knew that they had come within a hairsbreadth of disaster. They knew, too, that the war had left them the legacy of a serious problem, and that a people both exhaused by the conflict and jubilant at the prospect of luxuriating in peace and prosperity would have little enthusiasm for dealing with it.

III

The problem was the public debt, the high price of Independence. This debt was owed both at home and abroad. The foreign debt amounted to more than $11,000,000, and would have to be paid in specie or its equivalent. Since the nation's principal foreign creditor had agreed to forego interest payments until 1787,[34] and Dutch bankers seemed willing to pick up interest charges on what remained, there was little urgency here. The domestic debt was a more pressing and complex problem.

Most of the foreign debt had been contracted by one government, namely Congress. The domestic debt had been contracted by fourteen different governments, and the largest debt by far had been contracted by a government which lacked the power to tax. Herein lay an additional source of confusion. In the absence of revenue-raising powers, the only way Congress could pay its debt was to parcel it out among the states. Congress had also contracted debts with and made advances to the various states. To the extent that any given state had exerted itself in furthering the common cause, as determined by Congress, it was entitled to a credit against the continent. This would have to be taken into consideration in any final settlement of accounts between the states and Congress in which credits would be balanced against debits. It would also affect whether a state emerged as net debtor or net creditor.[35]

If the process of setting these matters straight sounds complicated in the abstract, it was infinitely more so in the excution. For a start, how could one deal with the different values accorded to the money, goods, and services subscribed at different times throughout the war? The depreciation forced both the continent and the states to "liquidate" their respective debts; that is, to reduce them to common specie value according to depreciation tables compiled for the course of the war. From 1782 on, they tried most earnestly to do so, and a fairly accurate estimate of the liquidated federal debt was available by early 1783.[36] It included the moneys subscribed to the Continental loan office, the final settlement notes issued to the Army upon its disbanding, and the certificate debt deriving from the impressment of supplies, mostly in the Hudson Valley area. The most widely held form of debt, Continental bills of credit of the old and new emission, were conspicuously excluded from the liquidated federal debt, the latter because they had always been considered the responsibility of the states, the former because their rapid circulation while depreciating was thought to have acted as equitably as a tax might have in retiring them.[37]

Liquidation was only a first, though necessary, step in attacking the problem of the debt. One also had to make provision for paying it. Payment, however, was not high in the priorities of a vast majority of the population in the immediate postwar period. Having been denied easy access to foreign imports throughout the war, Americans tended to go on a spending spree with the announcement of peace. Moreover, the temporary rise in the price of American produce in relation to European imports that accompanied the peace impelled many to spend in advance of income and to expand private indebtedness.[38] Those pressed by private debts did not relish the prospect of assuming the burden of public ones as well, and it is not surprising that many of the state legislatures proved hostile either to providing fully for their own state debts or to complying with Congress' requisitions.

There were exceptions. In 1782 a Massachusetts public creditor interest succeeded in funding a significant part of that state's unusually large debt, in appreciating its market value to close to 33 percent of its liquidated value, and in maintaining it at that level so that it could serve as a source of capital.[39] Massachusetts first showed how a public debt could be made to function as an asset as well as a liability, and thus help to provide for its own retirement by stimulating economic development, but only if the people had the virtue to raise sufficient revenue to pay interest

on the nominal sum in specie and thus ensure the ready nego-
tiability of the certificates.

Massachusetts succeeded in raising the necessary specie with
a state impost and excise, two indirect taxes whose collection took
place predominantly in areas that benefitted most from the partial funding of the debt and whose yields obligingly expanded in
the immediate postwar boom. Later, New York succeeded in fully
funding both its state debt and the Continental debt held by its
citizens. It enjoyed unique advantages in doing so. Though the
state had suffered grievously during the war from the enemy's
occupation of its wealthiest areas, it had nonetheless managed to
keep its debt down due to the continuous presence of the Continental Army in its midst, and in the immediate postwar period
the yield from its impost rose as its commerce expanded. By 1786
its new, consolidated debt was selling above par.[40] Pennsylvania
followed a similar course to New York, exploiting the windfall
from the avalanche of imports that came cascading into the port
of Philadelphia.[41] But other areas of the nation which had large
debts in relation to available resources and lacked a lucrative
impost fared less well.

Connecticut's experience illustrated some of the difficulties
that might be encountered. Lacking a vigorous import trade and
thus a convenient way to fund the debt by raising revenues
through indirect taxation, the state had the alternative of trying
to do this through direct taxation or settling for making certificates of the public's liquidated indebtedness receivable in satisfaction of taxes. The state's political system had emerged from the
war too shaken to pursue the former expedient, and the latter
insured that that debt would circulate at a fraction of liquidated
value if it circulated at all.[42] In effect the state's revenue shortage
deprived its people of a source of capital sorely needed to finance
postwar reconstruction. Under the circumstances, it was understandable and perhaps even desirable that the legislature reso-
lutely refuse to do anything for the federal creditors in its midst.
While it could not deny that their claims were as compelling as
those of the state creditors, it could nonetheless put them off by
pointing to the state's diminished resources and by arguing that,
since Connecticut was undoubtedly well in advance of the other
states in its contributions to the common cause, federal creditors
should wait until the final settlement of accounts between the
states before they were paid.[43] And Connecticut was by no means

the only state that found itself in straitened circumstances at the conclusion of the war.

The Revolutionary debt, then, hung like a millstone around the necks of all but a few of the most favored states in the immediate postwar period. And the disparity between the circumstances of the fortunate few and the less fortunate many compounded the problem by ensuring that federal requisitions would not be complied with. Those who enjoyed a privileged position in the postwar economy preferred to assume and service the outstanding obligations of their own citizens, both local and federal. They hoped that they would eventually be compensated in a final settlement and that in the interim they would enjoy the advantage to be derived from the availability of that much more capital in their domestic economies. Those in a less privileged position had no choice but to favor domestic over federal creditors or forfeit all the advantages that might be derived from funding at least some of the debt, as was the case with Massachusetts. And those with the least resources, like Connecticut, had to settle either for making some token satisfaction to domestic creditors that deprived them of most of the economic advantages from doing so, or to default entirely on their obligations. They certainly did not think rigorous compliance with federal requisitions should be at the top of their priorities. That meant that the federal government had nothing to pay interest with on the debt it was recognizing through the gradual process of liquidation except additional bills of credit unbacked by any solid resource. Though Congress gave them a special name, indents, and special status in its requisitions on the states in the hope of creating some demand for them in the marketplace, they went the way all unfunded paper instruments had gone since the early years of the war, dramatizing the continued difficulty the nation experienced in establishing any semblance of public credit.[44]

Nor, as time went on, was there much reason to expect that things might improve. For as the Revolutionary debt depreciated it increasingly became a speculative asset. The only people who would buy it were those with sufficient capital both to absorb a potential loss and patient enough to wait for a possible gain. Inevitably these people constituted a shrinking minority, as the difficult postwar economic adjustments progressively forced the vast majority to liquidate whatever assets they had in the effort to free themselves from both personal and public indebtedness.

Fewer and fewer public creditors were confronting more and more public debtors.[45] In a popular political system, such a development posed a lethal threat to public credit in general. What prevented the majority of public debtors from pointing to the fact that the Revolutionary debt was no longer held by those with whom it had initially been contracted, that this "sacred obligation" had instead been bought up by the wealthy few at vastly reduced prices, and that, paying it off at par would constitute an injustice perpetrated on the many exclusively for the benefit of the few? Such arguments began to surface early in the Confederation period and showed no signs of losing their cogency as time went on.[46]

IV

By now many readers must be wondering why the nation's leaders did not conclude that the best course was a general repudiation. If the public creditors were becoming such a small minority and their equitable claims on the public seemed increasingly dubious, what would have been lost by sacrificing their interests to those of the overwhelming majority? Forcing the minority to yield to the wishes of the majority was certainly congruent with the nation's republicanism, and would the Revolution not remain true to itself if such a route were pursued? Certainly voices were heard in this period that argued as much. But they remained the distinct minority, at least among that part of the population who engaged in formal political debate in the public prints. The vast majority agreed on the need to preserve public credit, and it is worth asking why that should have been the case, given the enormous obstacles that existed to doing so.

There was, of course, a simple, instrumental explanation for their apparent agreement. No one had had a chance to forget the war experience yet, and no one could ignore the difficulties that the Republic had experienced as a consequence of the loss of public credit. At the same time it was clear that Britain's capacity to sustain her public credit had been the principal reason why she had been able to persevere in a struggle that aligned her against most of the major maritime powers of Europe. If the United States had enjoyed the same advantage, she never would have been forced to rely on France to the extent that she did. If the

United States wanted to be independent in anything more than name, it behooved her to establish and nurture what experience had demonstrated was the most eligible means of maintaining access to the marketplace in time of war and to make sure she retained the capacity to organize the nation's resources through consensual means that were uniquely congruent with her republicanism rather than through force.[47]

Though no one who had occupied a responsible position during the war could have emerged from the experience without having such instrumental concerns on their mind, I am not sure they were decisive in the so-called "critical period." After all, the nation was at peace, and though she was subject to repeated humiliations at the hands of European nations during these years, there seemed to be no disposition on the part of the major powers to embroil the United States in a new war. So an immediate repudiation of the remaining war debt would not necessarily have compromised the Republic's security in the distant future, particularly if care had been taken to reestablish some form of credit in the interval so as to convince potential lenders that the Revolutionary repudiation would not be a precedent for the future. Had steps not already been taken in the direction of a partial repudiation by allowing more than $200,000,000 of the Continental currency to depreciate out of existence? Since perfect justice was impossible under the circumstances, why not admit as much and start from scratch? Indeed, from a purely instrumental view this plan looked like the preferred course, since it offered a better prospect of having some form of public credit established before it was next needed.

But to have followed such a policy would have undercut the elaborate procedures that Congress and most of the states had been pursuing since 1781 to liquidate and settle their accounts on equitable principles, both with their individual creditors and with each other. And this complex process, from which some definition of public justice would emerge, involved the essence, rather than a dispensable excrescence, of republicanism. Credit for us is an impersonal concept. Though occasionally we borrow from people we know, most of the credit extended and accepted comes from institutions. If we fail to pay our debts, we are not wronging our friends but simply defaulting on an impersonal, legal obligation which is likely to have no perceptible effect on the agency that extended the loan. In the eighteenth century, most credit was of an intensely personal kind, tendered by individuals to other individuals in face-to-face agreements. Moreover, in a currency-shy economy, this kind of personal credit was pervasive; it was, if you will, the cement of society where each pledged his faith to others. Those who did not have money to lend could nonetheless lend produce or services. If one looks at the individual account books of people from all walks of life in this period, one is struck by how little space is occupied by cash exchanges in them and how extensive book debts were. In the same way, neighbors and friends customarily endorsed each other's notes to distant third parties to give them a credit worthiness. Not infrequently the financial failure of a friend or neighbor might involve a perfectly innocent individual in serious economic difficulties. But under normal circumstances, such endorsements were considered to be one of the routine obligations of neighborliness. Credit for eighteenth-century Americans, then, meant more than access to someone else's money; it also referred to a network of trust that was one of the basic lineaments of society.[18]

Since, at the time, people were less experienced with public credit than with private credit, their ideas about the latter inescapably influenced their expectations about the former. If the public defaulted on its obligations to private individuals, it would destroy the basic trust which should exist between the Republic and the individual, particularly since the society at large could not plead the excuse that private bankrupts sometimes could, of being without sufficient resources. The Republic's assets were in principle the sum total of the people's wealth, and while the debt remained smaller than society's total assets, there was no excuse to plead bankruptcy and every reason to offer justice to the creditor.[49] How else could a republic cohere except around a common interest? And what better focus existed for the loyalties of all than common justice, a principle that seemed to rise above individual biases and to offer a transcendent and secure foundation for common agreement. On the other hand, if the public repudiated its debt to individuals, it would justifiably alienate them from a government whose strength was thought to depend on the support of all, and in this case it would be alienating precisely those people who had the most resources with which to support the commonwealth. Such a policy seemed both immoral and imprudent.[50]

So it is not surprising that calls for outright repudiation were seldom heard, and, where they were, they usually met with blistering rebuttal.[51] Much more prevalent in the immediate aftermath of the war were policies that involved covert repudiation. Popular majorities in the state legislatures increasingly resorted to such policies as stay laws and paper money issues. With the former they obstructed the capacity of private creditors to pay their share of the public debt and with the latter they sought to create a depreciating medium through which public obligations could be retired with relative ease.

No wonder certain elements in the Revolutionary leadership were disturbed by these developments. Thomas Paine, attempting to resist such tendencies, had pleaded that a republic embodied the sovereignty of justice rather than that of will.[52] And Madison, in a famous document entitled "The Vices of the Political System . . . ," complained bitterly of the irresponsible behavior that the legislatures, filled by debtor majorities, were increasingly displaying as the decade progressed.[53] When, in his famous *Federalist* No. 10, Madison referred to faction as a *majority* or a minority combined to pursue interests "adverse to the rights of other citizens, or to the permanent and aggregate interests of the community," he had the threat a debtor majority posed to a creditor minority foremost in his mind.[54]

Madison's solution, and one shared by many others, was to strengthen the central government. The solution had several things to recommend it. First a central government would to some extent screen out the less capable from active participation in national politics, much as the old imperial polity had placed a premium on an elite leadership.[55] Secondly, a central government could lay a uniform impost in such a way as to ensure that it would raise the maximum revenue. So long as the states levied separate imposts, the yields were bound to be compromised, because each state would compete with the others to attract trade.[56] The impost, in turn, was regarded as the most important source of revenue, because one could raise precious hard coin needed to pay interest on the funded debt and to appreciate it into a capital asset without fear of sparking a tax rebellion. The impost was paid by the merchant when he imported goods into the United States and was then passed along to consumers in the price of those goods. Not only was it a hidden tax, but no one paid it who didn't wish to buy the goods. In this particular case everyone who contributed to the revenue explicitly consented to do so in a way that was not the case when legislatures laid direct taxes.[57] But a strengthened federal government would have to have greater powers than those of laying an impost because the states were unlikely to part with this preferred form of revenue willingly or to let it yield anything unless the federal government agreed to assume responsibility for at least some of the state debts.[58] In other words, it was unlikely an impost by itself, that Congress under the Articles of Confederation had been vainly seeking since 1781, would solve the problem. What was necessary was an entirely new national government.

Such a radical departure from the way in which the Revolutionary enterprise had hitherto been conducted could not but encounter resistance. Quite apart from the debtor majorities that were emerging in the state legislatures, many had vested interests in a system that favored local power over central power. For instance, the small states, who received equal representation with the large states under the Articles of Confederation, knew perfectly well that the large states would not agree to a stronger, central government unless they were given proportional representation in it. Thus, agreeing to a major constitutional revision threatened to reduce the smaller states' influence in the nation's counsels.[59] Nor were the larger states entirely free of similar fears. The second largest state in the confederation, Massachusetts, illustrates their dilemma.

Virginia and Massachusetts had acted as uneasy partners throughout the Revolution, each vying with the other for leadership. Though considerably smaller than her Southern rival, Massachusetts had managed to maintain her influence through the development of innovative public policies that commanded respect by the manner in which they addressed outstanding problems. Her success in partially funding her large domestic debt during 1782 was a recent case in point. But since she was only a little more than a half as large as Virginia, she too had as much reason to fear the loss of influence to an arrogant Southern aristocracy as did the smaller states.[60] In fact, until the Articles of Confederation could be proved to be hopelessly ill-equipped in coping with the principal problem that the nation faced, revision was unlikely and attempts at replacement futile.

That is why Shays' Rebellion in 1788 became the critical event of the "critical period." The rebellion had grown out of the conjuncture of a large congressional requisition with the trade contraction of 1785. The diminished imports that accompanied the liquidity crisis of that year, as consumers tried to retire their outstanding indebtedness, had reduced the yields of the state's impost and excise to a point that placed the funding policy of 1782 in jeopardy. The only way that specie could continue to be raised to pay interest on the state debt was through direct taxation. But the only way to command the necessary majority in the legislature to accomplish this end was to place the federal creditors in a similar condition to the state ones by complying with Congress' requisition. That meant embarking on a heroic policy of direct taxation for specie which led at least part of the debtor majority in the state to rise in arms and attempt to close down the court system through which both private debts and public taxes would be collected.[61]

The creditor interest in Massachusetts could not have been unaware of the risks they were taking with the course they pursued. But they were impelled to do it by several considerations, the most important of which was the desire of the Massachusetts leadership to reassert their vanguard position in the confederation. They hoped to use what were thought to be the special strengths of their uniquely republican constitution to show that the decentralized route to establishing public credit could be made to work if only the individual states exerted sufficient political virtue.[62]

The spectacle of the second largest state in the confederation, and the one that possessed the most legitimate republican constitution, erupting in armed rebellion in response to an effort to comply with a congressional requisition while maintaining its own funding scheme, was all that it took to get the other states, with the exception of Rhode Island, to name delegations to the Philadelphia Convention. If Massachusetts' attempts to blaze a state route to establishing public credit could come to such dramatic grief, other less advantageously situated states would inevitably find themselves in similar difficulties and the Revolutionary War debt, the honoring of which alone could provide a secure basis for the republic, would necessarily go forfeit. The Philadelphia Convention assembled in response to the demonstrated inability of the states by themselves to solve the major, unresolved problem left over from the Revolutionary War.

Revolutionary leaders also recognized that postponing its resolution might make it impossible ever to solve. The first principal payments on the foreign debt were about to come due,[63] and though more European loans might be procured to forestall this crisis, they were unlikely to be forthcoming if the spectacle of Shays' Rebellion were allowed to stand uncorrected. Moreover, the process of repressing the Shaysites in Massachusetts had done little for the state's finances or her capacity to renew her efforts either to pay her own debts or those of the continent. While the state debt dramatically increased as a consequence of the military occupation of its western region, a popular reaction against the repression manifested itself in the May elections to the General Court which brought to the capital a legislative majority hostile to the vanguardism that had touched off the rebellion.[64] If justice was to be done the public creditors and the most influential people in the nation were not to be alienated from a republican order, some decisive action had to be taken and quickly.

V

The Philadelphia Convention did more than simply create a government that could make provision for the payment of the Revolutionary War debt. The Framers seized the occasion to implement much of the wisdom that had been accumulated both in running republican regimes and framing republican constitutions since 1775 when they drafted a new form of government that they hoped would be equipped to confront every contingency. But solving the problem of the debt remained their critical concern. This was evident on June 19 when the fateful decision was made to reject the New Jersey plan and proceed with the Virginia plan of government, regardless of the latter's reliance on proportional representation. The New Jersey plan had been hastily contrived by some of the delegates from the smaller states in an effort to retain as much of the confederation form of government as possible, at the same time empowering Congress to raise a uniform impost and to regulate trade. Its rejection signaled that the Convention was unprepared to risk any more half measures and that they realized a uniform impost might not be sufficient to solve the problem posed by the debt. Though more state delegations had reason to fear loss of influence in a new government based on the principle of proportional representation than to welcome it because it might increase their power, an overwhelming majority of the states made this choice because they realized it alone would provide the kind of government needed to solve their most pressing problem.[65]

The same logic affected the ratification controversy. The sponsors of the new government faced an uphill fight, even when they employed a strategy of referring the document to popularly elected ratifying conventions. Six of the conventions called contained Antifederalist majorities, and half of these represented states the new government could not do without, namely Massachusetts, New York, and Virginia. Yet the Federalists triumphed over their opponents in all but one of the six, namely North Carolina. Recent scholarship has focused on the manipulative strategies employed by the Federalists in the conventions, their success in narrowing the issue down to amending before or after ratification, and the pressures they brought to ensure the latter course be pursued.[66] But the situation that the Antifederalists found themselves in acted as an equally powerful persuader. The critics of the proposed new form of government had no alternative to offer. The political order they attempted to defend had not solved the problem of the Revolutionary debt and demonstrably could not. They were thus left in the unenviable situation of either surrendering to the Federalists or assuming responsibility for the shipwreck of a republic for which they had sacrificed as much as their adversaries had. It was precisely because everyone had an interest in establishing the public credit of the new nation, not just those who owned the securities, as Beard thought, that the Constitution was eventually ratified, the new government successfully implemented, and most important of all, a comprehensive plan for funding both the federal and a major part of the state debts adopted.

Beard's seminal insight in his *An Economic Interpretation* lay in his perception of the crucial role played by the Revolutionary War debt in the drafting and adoption of the Constitution. Both he and Hofstadter failed to understand what that role was, though. Hofstadter's interests lay elsewhere and he never paid much attention to the problem. With Beard the difficulty lay in his failure to realize that debtor and creditor, in the public and private sectors, have complementary as well as opposed interests; the debtors, after all, need money to borrow, and the creditors need enterprising people to put their capital to work. The events of the immediate postwar period had highlighted the divergence of interest between debtors and creditors. It was the genius of Hamilton's fiscal policy to transform this situation into one in which the community of interests between both again became apparent to each. He did so by opening a federal loan to which creditors were willing to subscribe their certificates of indebtedness and on which the public was both able and willing to pay interest charges.[67]

More than anything else, Hamilton's brilliant policies established the authority of the new government by their stunning resolution of the most intractable problem left over from the war. In doing so they began a tradition which is perhaps as important as the Constitution itself to the preservation of our liberty. In a free society authority should be reserved for persons and institutions that succeed in solving a nation's outstanding problems in a manner to which free men and women can readily consent.

Notes

1. Quotes here and below from Charles A. Beard, *An Economic Interpretation of the Constitution* (New York, 1935), 324–25.

2. As quoted in Ellen Nore, *Charles A. Beard: An Intellectual Biography* (Carbibdale and Edwardsville, Ill., 1983), 83; also Richard Hofstadter, *The Progressive Historians: Turner, Beard, Parrington* (Chicago, 1988), 212.

3. Hofstadter, *Progressive Historians*, 212.

4. These are noted in Maurice Blinkoff, "The Influence of Charles A. Beard on American Historiography," *University of Buffalo Studies* vol. 12, no. 4 (1938), 17.

5. Ibid., 37–38.

6. Taken from Nore, *Charles A. Beard*, 63, quoting from an anonymous review in the *Education Review*.

7. Ibid.

8. Ibid., 64.

9. Ibid., 65.

10. This is the interpretation of the book's reception developed by Hofstadter in Howard K. Beale, ed., *Charles A. Beard: An Appraisal* (Lexington, Ky., 1954), 87–88.

11. Ibid.; Maurice Blinkoff, "Influence of Beard," 31, 38, 38–47.

12. Hofstadter in Beale, ed., *Beard*, 90–91.

13. Hofstadter, *Progressive Historians*, 213.

14. The full title of Brown's book is *Charles Beard and the Constitution: A Critical Analysis of "An Economic Interpretation of the Constitution"* (Princeton, N.J., 1958); and of McDonald's is *We the People: The Economic Origins of the Constitution* (Chicago, 1958).

15. McDonald, *We The People*, 43–44, 58.

16. Ibid., 91–92; quote 109.

17. Ibid., 100, 108.

18. Ibid., 350–53.

19. Ibid., 355.

20. The strategy had first been used in *The American Political Tradition* (New York, 1948) and, in relation to Beard, had first been deployed in his essay "Charles Beard and the Constitution," which appeared in Beale, ed., *Beard*, 83ff.

21. Hofstadter, *Progressive Historians*, 216–18.

22. Ibid., 243.

23. Quote from ibid., 245; see also 230, 235.

24. Gordon S. Wood, *The Creation of the American Republic* (Chapel Hill, 1969), ch. 2, especially 6ff, celebrates this theme.

25. J. G. A. Pocock, *The Machiavellian Moment* (Princeton, N.J., 1976), is largely responsible for the fashion of such an inference, see ch. 11, 454, 460–61.

26. The story is told in my *Dear Liberty: Connecticut's Mobilization for the Revolutionary War* (Middletown, Ct., 1980), passim.

27. E. James Ferguson, *The Power of the Purse* (Chapel Hill, 1967), followed a long tradition in pursuing this interpretation.

28. See Richard Buel, Jr., "Samson Shorn: The Impact of the Revolutionary War on Estimates of the Republic's Strength," in Ronald Hoffman and Peter J. Albert, eds., *Arms and Independence: The Military Character of the American Revolution* (Charlottesville, Va., 1984), 155–56.

29. Ibid., 158, 160.

30. Richard Buel, Jr., "The Public Creditor Interest in Massachusetts Politics 1780–1786," 3 (given at Historic Deerfield, November 16, 1986 and forthcoming in the Proceedings of the Conference on Shays' Rebellion sponsored by Historic Deerfield and Amherst College).

31. *Dear Liberty* makes reference to some of these as well as to the overall workings of a provincial tax system.

32. See Buel, *Dear Liberty*, 165ff.

33. Lee Kennett, *The French Forces in America, 1780–1783* (Westport, Ct., 1977), 68.

34. See Hunter Miller, ed., *Treaties and other Acts of the United States of America* (Washington, D.C., 1931–1948), 2:48–56.

35. The best discussion of this complicated process in the secondary literature is to be found in Ferguson, *Power of the Purse*, ch. 10.

36. Worthington C. Ford, ed., *Journals of the Continental Congress, 1774–1789* (Washington, D.C., 1904–1937), 14:285–86.

37. See Ferguson, *Power of the Purse*, 67.

38. See James Madison to Edmund Randolph, February 11, 1783, to James Madison, Sr., February 12; also Edmund Randolph to Madison, April 14, Madison to Randolph, May 13, Joseph Jones to Madison, May 31, and Edmund Pendleton to Madison, June 2, in William T. Hutchinson and William M. E. Rachal, eds., *The Papers of James Madison* (Chicago, 1962–   ), 6:224, 229, 461; 7:42–43, 99, 106.

39. Buel, "The Public Creditor Interest," 5–6.

40. Forrest McDonald, *E Pluribus Unum: The Formation of the American Republic 1776–1790* (Boston, 1965), 59–61; also Ezekiel Cornell to Nicholas Brown, January 29, 1787, in Brown Papers, John Carter Brown Library.

41. McDonald, *E Pluribus Unum*, 51.

42. See Buel, *Power of Purse*, 322–23.

43. Ibid., 318–19.

44. Ferguson, *Power of Purse*, 223–29.

45. Ibid., ch. 12.

46. See, for instance, "Free Republican" 4 in *Independent Chronicle*, December 22, 1785 and "Public Faith" from a Springfield, Mass., paper, reprinted in *Massachusetts Centinel*, February 8, and *Independent Chronicle*, February 16, 1786.

47. See "Honestus" and "Solon" in *Independent Chronicle*, March 10, 1785; "Speech of a member of the General Court of Massachusetts," *American Museum* 1 (1787): 360.

48. See Gordon S. Wood, "Interest and Disinterestedness in the Making of the Constitution," in Richard Beeman, Stephen Botein, and Edward C. Carter II, eds., *Beyond Confederation: Origins of the Constitution and American National Identity* (Chapel Hill, 1987), 106–07.

49. See, for instance, Nathaniel Hazard, *Observations on the Peculiar Case of the Whig Merchants* (New York, 1785), 13–14.

50. See George Washington to John Jay, May 18 and August 1, 1786, in John C. Fitzpatrick, ed., *The Writings of George Washington* (Washington, D.C., 1931–1944), 28:431–32, 503. Also Alexander Hamilton, "To the Public Creditors of the State of New York," September 30, 1782 in Harold C. Syrett, ed., *The Papers of Alexander Hamilton*, (New York, 1961–1979), 3:176; also Hamilton to Wash-

ington, April 8, 1783 in *Papers of Hamilton*, 318, 320 and his "Remarks on an Act Granting to Congress Certain Imposts and Duties," and "Remarks on Equality of Representatives of the States in Congress" in *Papers of Hamilton*, 4:91–92; also James Madison, "Notes on Debates," February 21 and February 27, 1783 in Hutchinson and Rachal, eds., *Papers of James Madison*, 6:272, 298; also "Congress's Address to the States," April 25, 1783 in *Papers of Madison*; and Thomas Jefferson to James Madison, June 20, 1787 in *Papers of Madison*, 10:64.

51. See, for instance, the reception "Public Faith," which appeared in *Massachusetts Centinel*, February 8, 1786, met with in "A Friend to the Community", *Papers of Madison*, February 11; "An American," in *Papers of Madison*, February 18; and "A.B.," in *Papers of Madison*, February 22.

52. Thomas Paine, "Dissertation on Government: the Affairs of the Bank and Paper Money," in William M. van der Weyde, ed., *The Life and Works of Thomas Paine* (New Rochelle, N.Y., 1925), 4:234.

53. "Vices of the Political system of the U. States," in Gaillard Hunt, ed., *The Writings of James Medison* (New York, 1901), 2:366–67.

54. Jacob E. Cooke, ed., *The Federalist* (Cleveland, Ohio, 1961), 57.

55. This theme has been celebrated in Wood, *Creation of the American Republic*, ch. 12, especially 506ff.

56. "Policy of Connecticut III," *Connecticut Courant*, March 9, 1784.

57. "Policy of Connecticut II," *Connecticut Courant*, March 2, 1784.

58. See, for instance, "Proceedings of the [Middletown] Convention," in *Connecticut Courant*, March 30, 1784.

59. See Madison's speech before the Convention in *Papers of Madison*, 5:59–60, 80, 96, 100–01.

60. See Stephen Higginson to John Adams, July 1786 in J. Franklin Jameson, ed., "Letters of Stephen Higginson, 1783–1804" in *Annual Report of the American Historical Association for the Year 1896* (Washington, D.C., 1897), 1:734–35.

61. I have told this story in "The Public Creditor Interest in Massachusetts Politics," 8ff.

62. Ibid., 11

63. See ante #34.

64. See James Madison to George Washington, April 16, to Edmund Pendleton, April 22, to Thomas Jefferson, April 23, and to James Monroe, April 30, 1787 in Hutchinson and Rachal, eds., *Papers of Madison*, 11:386–87, 397, 398–99, 408. Also Stephen Higginson to Henry Knox, February 13, 1787 and to Nathan Dane, June 3, 1787 in Jameson, ed., "Letters of Higginson," 751, 756.

65. Only eleven states participated in this vote, Rhode Island and New Hampshire being unrepresented. Though the idea of balancing proportional representation of population in one House with equal representation of the states in another, subsequently known as the great compromise, had already been raised in the Convention, it had initially been rejected. The states that opposed proceeding on the basis of the Virginia plan were two of the smaller states, Delaware and New Jersey, and New York, which had already succeeded in providing for all its creditors, both state and federal.

66. Linda G. DePauw, *The Eleventh Pillar: New York State and the Federal Constitution* (Ithaca, N.Y., 1966).

67. The best overall account remains Ferguson, *Power of the Purse*, chs. 13 and 14; also Richard Buel, Jr., *Securing the Revolution* (Ithaca, N.Y., 1972), ch. 1.

America and the Creation of the Revolutionary Intellectual World of the Enlightment

by

Jack P. Greene

I

One has only to read through some of the correspondence of the generation that created an independent American nation to appreciate the high levels of activity and energy, the exuberant spirit of empirical inquiry, and the expansive optimism that characterized the American intelligentsia during the half century after the Declaration of Independence. Along with a confident faith in a future limited only by the extent of man's ingenuity, these qualities of that generation's approach to life and to the world about them gave them a mentality that will seem to most of us strikingly modern. So similar indeed is the orientation of that generation to our own that it has been difficult for mid-twentieth-century people to appreciate how revolutionary it was within the context of the development of western thought and culture. But this outlook was in fact something quite new, something quite uncharacteristic of earlier generations, and it constituted a fundamental transformation in the nature of human expectations about the world and about mankind, a transformation that, occurring during the late eighteenth century, was significantly accelerated by the specifically American developments of that time.

"Realistic yet hopeful, scientific but humanist, respectful but secular, trusting in institutions yet treating them as provisional, and looking to the day when all men [would be] . . . autonomous," the "inquisitive, liberating, intellectually adventurous frame of mind" exhibited by so many Americans of that time held out new hope for mankind. Confident that reason and science would lead them to an ever fuller understanding of the world, they believed that that understanding would permit people to become active agents in a wholesale reconstruction of their social environments and of the social institutions that governed them. In this new world, passive acceptance of authority would be replaced by an active spirit of free critical inquiry; tradition and a respect for the past would give way to an orientation toward the future; a social system characterized by hierarchy, ascription, dependence, and exploitation would yield to one emphasizing equality, merit, personal independence, human fraternity, and social benevolence; a human condition dominated by failure, frustration, despair, and misery would be wiped away in favor of one characterized by opportunity, achievement, fulfillment, and happiness—a world of limits, in short, would be replaced by one that knew no bounds.[1]

Borrowing a term from the times, cultural historians refer to this "great revolution in man's thinking that came to dominate the Western world in the eighteenth century" as the Enlightenment, and they have generally explained it as a development that had its origins almost wholly within Europe. Thus, Peter Gay, the most influential recent American student of the Enlightenment, has traced it to a series of largely internal European developments—"the triumph of Newtonian science, striking improvements in industrial and agricultural techniques, a widespread loss of religious fervor and a corresponding rise of 'reasonable' religion, an ever bolder play of the critical spirit among the old mysteries of church and state which had for centuries escaped criticism, [and] a new sense of confidence in man's power over his wordly destiny." Although Gay and most other students of the Enlightenment have not denied that the creation of the American federal republic between 1776 and 1788 both accelerated and was widely regarded as one of the outstanding achievements of the Enlightenment, they seem generally to agree that in formulating the ideas and expectations of the Enlightenment the "American colonists [and colonies] had no part." Indeed, students of the American phase of the Enlightenment, including Donald H. Meyer and Henry F. May, have had no trouble in accepting the judgments of European historians that the American Enlightenment was provincial and derivative, that the "Americans were consumers, depending heavily, almost exclusively, on borrowings from overseas," that American philosophers like Franklin, Jefferson, Adams, and Madison were "apt and candid disciples" who "went to school to a handful of European thinkers."[2]

In this essay, I want not so much to challenge this view but to look in a frankly playful and highly speculative way at the American relationship to the intellectual transformation of the late eighteenth century from a somewhat different—and much longer—perspective. Specifically, I want here to explore the extent to which America first helped to inspire and then came to epitomize the transformation in the character of human expectations during the early modern era.

This is not a subject that has been widely canvased. As J. H. Elliott has remarked, historians have mostly assumed that Europe's impact on the rest of the world, including America, was of much "greater interest and concern than the impact of the world on Europe." Not only, most historians seem to agree, did other important developments—the revival of interest in antiquity associated with the Renaissance, the so-called educational and scientific revolutions, the Protestant Reformation, and the expansion of external trade both within Europe and between Europe and the Levant, Africa, America, and Asia—developments that were contemporary with the discovery and exploration of America—appear to have been more important in helping to stimulate different modes of thought and mental outlooks in the early modern era. The discovery of America, as several scholars have emphasized, appears to have "made relatively little impression on Europe" and, astonishing as it may now seem, to have "registered little impact on the values, beliefs, and traditions of the sixteenth and seventeenth centuries."[3] Notwithstanding these judgments, there are strong reasons to suspect that the role of America in contributing to stimulate changes in traditional mental outlooks from the early sixteenth century on has not yet been sufficiently appreciated.

II

As many scholars have pointed out, the New World of America was revealed to Europe not immediately upon discovery but only gradually over several centuries.[4] Within a quarter century after Columbus' first landing at San Salvador, however, Europeans understood two powerful truths about the land Columbus had encountered: first, that it was a genuinely new, that is, a previously unknown world, that was not, as Columbus initially hoped, part of the continent of Asia; and, second, that it was enormous. The newness of the New World was dramatically indicated by the hitherto unknown animals, plants, and peoples it contained and by the accounts of its peculiarities of climate and terrain, and these new aspects of the New World—in the words of the French philosopher Louis LeRoy, "new lands, new seas, new formes of men, manners, lawes, and customs; new diseases and new remedies; new waies of the Heavens, and of the Ocean, never before found out"—fired their imaginations and turned their attention more and more away from the Mediterranean and toward the Atlantic. But no aspect of the New World probably operated so powerfully in this regard as did its immense space. "The discovery of [such] a boundless country," declared Montaigne in the late 1570s, was indeed "worth[y of consideration."[5]

As the awareness of the seeming *boundlessness* of America penetrated more deeply into European consciousness, America, in the words of the Dutch historian Henri Baudet, became a place "onto which all identification and interpretation, all dissatisfaction and desire, all nostalgia and idealism seeking expression could be projected." "In observing America," Elliott has noted, Europe "was, in the first instance, observing itself." Throughout the middle ages, Europeans had posited the existence of a place—for a time to the east but mostly to the west of Europe—without the corruptions and disadvantages of the Old World. The discovery of America intensified this "nostalgia for the Golden Age and the Lost Paradise" and aroused new hope for their discovery somewhere on the western edge of the Atlantic.[6]

Remarkably soon after its discovery, in fact, America became the locus for a variety of "imaginary . . . utopian constructions." Indeed, the very term utopia was invented by Sir Thomas More in 1515–16 in his famous tract of that name. Although most students of More and of the utopian tradition put little emphasis upon it, More located Utopia in the Atlantic and used as his central literary device the experienced traveler just returned from the "unknown nations and countries" of the New World. As these facts and a close reading of his text also make clear, More was obviously inspired in this effort by the as yet unknown potential of the immense New World. Specifically, the discovery of

America—in all its vastness—suggested to More the heady possibility of *finding* a place where all the problems of a decadent Europe had either been resolved or had not yet been permitted to develop. Nor did this close association between America and the utopian tradition end with More. From More through Jonathan Swift and beyond, utopian writers continued to associate America with the dream of a perfect society and to locate their fairylands, their New Atlantis, their City of the Sun in some distant place in the vicinity of America.[7]

But these early utopias all looked backward to Europe's "own ideal past" rather than forward into some wholly novel world of the future: invariably, their authors turned their imaginary "new worlds into very old ones."[8] As we have learned from modern anthropologists, "knowledge of other cultures and eras [invariably] depends on the cultures and eras doing the knowing."[9] Thus, although early reports from the New World depicted America—in contrast to Europe, Africa, and Asia—"as a land of liberty, where the earth like the air belonged to all in common and where wealth, like the water of a river, was shared by all; [and] where there were none of the lawsuits engendered by the words Thine and Mine" and although, as William Brandon has recently argued, such reports may very well have eventually been a major stimulus for the development in early modern European thought of the entirely new—and modern—Enlightenment conception of liberty as equality and masterlessness, for over two centuries following Europe's encounter with the New World conventional preconceptions seem to have prevented all but a handful of European commentators from recommending the alleged liberty of the American Indians as a condition to be pursued by Europeans.[10] For that reason, it is obviously incorrect to suggest that the discovery of America immediately enabled the European "to picture himself as a free agent in the deep and radical sense of possessing unlimited possibilities in his own being, and as living in a world made by him in his own image and to his own measure."[11] Nevertheless, with its large unexplored areas and its many unfamiliar groups of people and cultures, America did provide the European with powerful additional impetus for the exertion of the critical spirit of Renaissance humanism and for posing basic questions about his own society and its organization, values, and customs. This is the context in which the utopian tradition in early modern Europe ought to be understood.

That tradition consisted of several types of utopias ranging from pastoral arcadias to perfect commonwealths to millennial kingdoms of God. Whatever their form, however, they all betrayed "deep dissatisfaction" with contemporary Europe and were intended, in More's words, as "patterns . . . for correcting the errors of these [European] nations among whom we live." Having, prior to the discovery of America, expressed this dissatisfaction in their "longing for a return to . . . the lost Christian paradise, or to the Golden Age of the ancients," Europeans now exchanged this desire for "a world remote in time" for one distant in space. Arcadia, Eden, the New Jerusalem, or the scientifically advanced and dominated Bensalem created by Francis Bacon, now could be plausibly located in America. In their good order, just government, supportive society, peaceful abundance, and absence of greed, vice, and private property, these happy social constructions, situated by their authors in the New World, served as the antithesis of the old.[12]

Although Europeans continued to locate their utopias in the unknown wilds of America, the dream of finding a perfect society somewhere in the physical spaces of America gradually lost force during the century from 1550 to 1650. As America and Americans came to be better known and as no such utopias were discovered, people realized that America, to the extent that it was known, was not an unalloyed paradise to be contrasted with a European hell. Scholars have written much about the fascination of European scholars with the exotic productions of America and in particular with the noble savages who inhabited it, and this interest should by no means be minimized. The tendency to glorify the Indians by depicting them as strong-limbed Greeks who, though pagan and simple, lived free with little labor and without regard for private property in a blissful state of nature was widespread.

But it existed in an uneasy state of tension with a still stronger impulse to emphasize what appeared to Europeans to be overwhelming evidence of European cultural superiority. Very few Europeans, in fact, seem to have been capable of appreciating the integrity and quality of Indian culture or not to have viewed America from a Europocentric perspective, and from that perspective the Indians, for all their supposed simple felicity, were neither Christian nor civilized but pagan and primitive, at most the equivalents of Europe's own early "rude inhabitants" prior to their conversion to Christianity and acquisition of civilized manners. Along with the relative ease of the European conquest, this perspective only helped to confirm Europeans in a deep sense of superiority and in the belief that Europe, for all its social and political warts, was, in the words of the late sixteenth-century English publicist Samuel Purchas, "the sole home of 'Arts and Inventions.' "[13]

Indeed, it was not only their contact with America that contributed to this sense of superiority. Developments within Europe were also important. In particular, the new science and technology associated with the scientific revolution—the growing use of the experimental method, the increased use of quantification and mathematics as a scientific tool, and a burgeoning interest in technology—led to scientific advances and technological achievements, especially in printing, warfare, and navigation, that seemed from a European point of view not only to put Europe miles ahead of even the most technologically advanced peoples encountered in America but also actually served as instruments for extending the "cultural and political influence of . . . Europe over all other parts of the globe." Although some of its leading exponents, Francis Bacon, Johann Valentin Andrae, and Tommaso Campanella, revealed through their utopian tracts an impatience with the rate of scientific discovery, the new achievements in science would, they confidently believed, ultimately lead to the betterment of mankind and the improvement of society.[14]

This urge for improvement was also manifest in a contemporary rage for projects and projecting that swept England, the Netherlands, and France beginning in the middle of the sixteenth century. Projects were schemes to introduce or improve old manufactures, crops, agricultural techniques, transportation, internal and external markets, and employment. These schemes were mostly designed with the intention of enriching their authors; but, taken together, they also acted, especially in England, to enrich society as a whole and to enhance the sense that material conditions and the quality of peoples' lives even at the lowest rungs of society were gradually getting more ample, if not necessarily better. The simultaneous expansion of commercial activity had much the same effect by stimulating and then catering to new levels of demand that ultimately seem to have brought levels of material prosperity in western Europe considerably higher than they had been earlier or than they were then among any of the native peoples of America.[15]

If the new science, many successful projects, and the expansion of commerce had enhanced Europe's sense of superiority over America after 1500, America itself came increasingly to be seen not simply as an exotic new land inhabited by primitives but as a place to be acted upon by Europeans, a place that was chiefly important for the new opportunities it provided for the mass conversion of souls to Christiantiy or, more commonly, for the acquisition of individual wealth. As America was "invested with the main chance," it was, increasingly "divested of magic." For the new European exploiters of America, the Indians came to seem far less like noble savages and far more like the Devil's children. What had initially seemed to be a paradise turned out to be a desert or a wilderness "haunted by demonic beings," infested with poisonous snakes and plants and vicious alligators, and subject to terrifying hurricanes and other inimical acts of nature. Indeed, in the conventional iconography of the time the allegorical figure of America was usually represented with an alligator which, as Hugh Honour has pointed out, quickly "aquire[d] a derogatory significance, especially when set beside Europe with her bull, Asia with her camel, and Africa with her lion."[16]

But it was not only the people, animals, plants, and natural phenomena that were native to America that gave it an ill fame but also the behavior of the Europeans who went there. In *Utopia*, More had worried whether "this discovery [of America], which was thought would prove so much to" the "advantage [of the discoverers, might] . . . by their imprudence become an occasion of much mischief to them." And that seemed to be precisely what had happened as, unable to control their lust for riches, the Spaniards had themselves turned savage in their wholesale exploitation and destruction of entire nations of Indian peoples. Not all the demons infesting America were American. Outside the bounds of traditional restraints, Europeans in America had permitted their most primitive instincts to trimph in their avid quest for individual gain, heedless of all civilized conventions and of all social and human costs. As this black legend of Spanish cruelty circulated widely through Europe during the late sixteenth century, America came more and more to be viewed as a place of cultural regress, for natives and immigrants alike, a place that was almost wholly barren of culture and that was important chiefly for the riches it yielded in such abundance for the benefit of a Europe that was the exclusive seat of civilized life.[17]

But riches were not the only thing that America exported to Europe during the sixteenth and seventeenth centuries. In his important and recently translated book *The Civilizing Process,* Norbert Elias has shown how, coincidental with the discovery and early exploration of America, Europeans were showing an ever greater concern for civility, a concern, he argues, that over the next three hundred years actually resulted in Europe's becoming more civilized.[18] Elias does not consider the possibility that the discovery of America might have had a role in this process. By providing Europeans with concrete examples of what they were not and did not want to become, however, greater and more extensive contacts with the so-called primitive peoples of America and elsewhere outside Europe seems to have required them to define more explicitly standards of what was and what was not *civilized* and thereby to have functioned as a powerful stimulus to this civilizing process. For Europeans continued to exhibit a powerful awareness that, whatever the extent of their vaunted cultural superiority over peoples elsewhere, they themselves often displayed, even within Europe itself, many of the same base and primitive characteristics that they attributed to Indians and to Europeans living in America. Thus, the new science, as Keith Thomas has shown in the case of England, coexisted with powerful undercurrents of belief in magic, witchcraft, astrology, and other forms of superstition.[19]

Perhaps more important, the new economic and religious conditions of the sixteenth and seventeenth centuries seemed to produce many unsettling side effects. The expansion of trade, the penetration of the market, the proliferation of joint-stock companies and the projecting spirit, the emergence of new and expanding forms of consumerism, and, toward the end of the seventeenth century, the development of a money economy complete with new financial institutions like the Bank of England and a mounting national debt undermined the traditional foundations of authority and stimulated new and extensively manifest forms of self-interested and egocentric economic, social, and political behavior. At the same time, the religious ferment associated with the Reformation, including especially the proliferation of a bewildering variety of sects and religious opinions, led to heightened religious discord, both civil and international war, and the shattering of the old unitary ecclesiastical order. In combination, these economic and religious developments evoked widespread anxieties that the old world was rapidly degenerating into a social and moral chaos.

Animated by these fears and nostalgic for the old order, a long line of social critics of radically different persuasions in England called, during the century and a half from 1575 to 1725, for a return to an older, more static, and more coherent social and religious order and to the traditional values of hierarchy, steward-ship, virtue, simplicity, thrift, moderation, and piety. This almost ubiquitous yearning for order, this pervasive persistence of con-ventional habits of thought, vividly indicates just how disquieting Englishmen found the steady acceleration of the pace of eco-nomic, social, and religious change that began under the Tudors and the extreme difficulty they had in discovering a vocabulary and patterns of perception appropriate to the changing condi-tions in which they lived. Although a few people, including John Locke, Bernard Mandeville, and several less well-known liberal economic writers tried to work out a rationale for the new socio-economic order, the logic of that new order was by and large obscured by nostalgia, and most social commentary from the Puritans through Filmer and Harrington to Bolingbroke and Swift betrayed a profound "desire for the renewal of old values and structures, the hope of a radical *renovation*," a "great instau-ration," that would once again restore coherence to the world.[20]

Nor were such impulses peculiar to England. A "traditional culture, suspicious of change and oriented to a mythic past, whose members fulfilled themselves in relationship to a divine reality outside time," early modern Europe was "a world that still sought its future in the past" and found it extremely difficult to come to terms with novelty. All of the great seventeenth-century upheavals in the Netherlands, France, Spain, and Italy, were, like the English Revolution of the 1640s and unlike the democratic revolutions at the end of the eighteenth century, "dominated, by the idea, not of progress, but of a return to a golden age in the past." Still holding to a theory of history that saw the past as either a providential design or a recurring cycle of advances and de-clines, they aspired to renovation, not innovation.[21]

Disappointed in their efforts to recapture the world they had lost in England, some men in the seventeenth century, like More a century earlier, turned to America as a place in which their objectives might be accomplished. In contrast to More, however, they thought in terms not of *finding* a preexistent utopia but of *founding* one in the relatively "empty" spaces of North America. Some Spaniards, the Jesuits with their theocratic *reductions* in Paraguay and Vasco de Quiroga with his communal religious villages in Santa Fe in New Spain, were already by the early seventeenth century striving to fashion utopias among groups of Indian peoples in America.[22]

But it was North America which had a far smaller and, in most places, considerably less settled aboriginal population than Hispanic America that seemed to offer the unlimited and, even more important, the as yet unoccupied and unorganized space in which a new society, free from the imperfections and restraints of the old, might be created. In dramatic contrast to the "civilized and filled space[s]" they had encountered in the Levant and the Orient, North America presented itself to Europeans as an immense, sparsely populated, and bounteous territory that was "open for experimentation." With "neither a history nor any political forms at all," it invited people to consider how in an as yet unarticulated space Old World institutions and socioeconomic, religious, and political arrangements might be modified to produce the best possible commonwealths. "In the beginning all the World was America," John Locke wrote in his *Second Treatise of Government*, and this conception of America as an unformed and "free space," a place still free from the corruptions and "trammels of the Old World" and waiting to be the site of Europe's new beginning, inspired English colonial organizers with the dream of creating through conscious instrumental human action and planning a New Jerusalem or a New Eden. If an existing paradise of the kind imagined by Sir Thomas More was not to be found in America, Englishmen now hoped to design and construct one in the wide open spaces of America.[23]

Shakespeare set out the formula by which this dream could be realized in 1611 in *The Tempest*, which was inspired by an actual wreck in Bermuda of an English ship bound for the new colony of Virginia. In that play, it will be recalled, Prospero, employing his superior European knowledge and skill, managed in little more than a decade to bring a civilized order out of the natural chaos of a virgin and only lightly occupied wilderness, in the process transforming it into "an idyllic land of ease, peace, and plenty." Beginning with the founding of Virginia in 1607, virtually every one of the new English colonies on the mainland and in the

Caribbean was to some extent animated by the hope of equalling Prospero's accomplishment. Over the succeeding century and a half, Anglo-North America seemed to offer a fertile soil for a large number of attempts to realize European dreams for the recovery of its own ideal past in a new carefully constructed society.[24]

Those attempts differed radically from one place to another. Puritan leaders in Massachusetts Bay and Connecticut hoped to establish the New Jerusalem in which, with God's help and their own considerable exertions, they would recreate the true church and live in Godly communion with one another in the millenial kingdom of God on Earth.[25] Lord Baltimore in Maryland and the Duke of York in New York hoped to establish the sort of well-ordered feudal societies that had not existed in England for at least a century and a half. James Harrington's semiutopian tract *Oceana* inspired the early plans for organizing the new colony of Carolina in the 1670s, and those plans, along with contemporary ones for New Jersey, were at least partly the work of Sir Anthony Ashley Cooper, First Earl of Shaftesbury, and his secretary John Locke. William Penn undertook a carefully planned holy experiment in Pennsylvania and Delaware in the 1680s, and fifty years later, in the 1730s, a group of humanitarian reformers established the new colony of Georgia as a model of social benevolence.[26] Despite their variety, all of these enterprises, no less than More's *Utopia*, exhibited a strong desire for the establishment of an ordered world, "an idealized version of old England," that would be without the problems and the anxieties of the metropolitan society.[27]

Of course, all of these efforts were failures. Indeed, with the exception of the Puritan experiment in New England which managed to perpetuate itself through the better part of two generations, their failures were almost immediate. In colony after colony, men discovered, to paraphrase a familiar aphorism, that you could take Englishmen out of England but you could not take England out of Englishmen, who did *not* lose their vices in the new soil of America. Yet, as John Murrin has pointed out, the "real significance" of the Anglo-American utopias lies not in their predictable failures but in the fact "that they were tried at all." For over a century, the unorganized space of North America had encouraged "some Englishmen to try out in practice" a great variety of religious, social, economic, and political ideas that could never have been attempted in the organized world of England itself.[28]

Notwithstanding their inability to realize or to sustain the utopian goals of their founders, moreover, all of the colonies—within a few decades in the case of the early ones and usually even sooner with most of the newer ones—did exceptionally well, and their economic, demographic, and territorial growth became the wonder not just of England but of all Europe. So rapid was their growth that they came to be known, in contrast to Old England and Continental Europe, as lands of abundance and opportunity in which men could enjoy plenty, independence, and freedom from the persecutions, the want, and the humiliating constraints of the crowded and constricted world from which they had come.[29]

Despite their spectacular and much envied growth, however, the Anglo-American colonies continued right down to the American Revolution to represent something of a disappointment, a disappointment not merely in terms of their inability to achieve their original utopian aspirations but also in terms of their failure to live up to or to achieve the standards of civilized development represented by Europe itself. As the creations of Europeans, these new settler societies in Anglo-America, created in the image of their creators, were "peculiarly the artefact of Europe, as Asia, Africa, and aboriginal America were not." For Europeans as well as for their descendants in America, that image was, moreover, as I emphasized earlier, the only legitimate image. European culture, the Mexican historian Edmundo O'Gorman has correctly argued, was never conceived of as one among many cultures but as "the only truly significant culture; European history was universal history. Europe became history's paradigm, and the European way of life [, whatever its defects,] came to be regarded [again, by Europeans and Euro-Americans,] as the supreme" standard by which the European societies in America were to be judged.

No less than the original native cultures, the new European colonies "could not be recognized and respected" in their own terms but could only expect to be considered complete when they had succeeded in transforming themselves into "a replica of the 'old' world." In colonies and metropolis alike, the primary hope,

the central aspiration, was not that the colonial societies would
come to terms with their environments but that, in the manner of
Prospero and, a century later, Robinson Crusoe, they would master and reorder those environments along European lines until,
as a result of a series of incremental improvements, they had
slowly moved from primitive simplicity to higher—and more
European—levels of cultural development. Indeed, in this colonial context, the term *improvement* was virtually interchangeable
with *European, English,* or *metropolitan.*[30]

Of this exalted standard, Britain's Anglo-American colonies,
however rapid and vigorous their growth throughout the first
seven decades of the eighteenth century, fell considerably short.
Many people on the Continent, including Voltaire and Montesquieu, and many more in Britain, admired the colonies for their
prosperity, freedom, and pastoral simplicity. But the crude, simple, undifferentiated, rural, and provincial nature of these societies, most of which were in large part built on the cruel exploitation of black people through an unremitting system of racial
slavery, and the impoverished and derivative character of their
artistic and intellectual life were so striking as to suggest to some
commentators, the most prominent of whom were the Comte de
Buffon and the Abbe Corneille de Pauw, that conditions in America were so unfavorable to life as to cause a marked physical,
mental, and moral degeneration among the creole (the native)
descendants of the Europeans. The same unfavorable compari-
sons of colonial America with metropolitan European cultures
underlay both a strong popular prejudice against and condescen-
sion toward the colonies in the Old World and a palpable sense of
inferiority and dependence among the colonists themselves.[31]

Thus, in America, no less than in England, did the constrain-
ing inheritance of the past operate powerfully to prevent people
from coming to terms with the present. The sense of openness
and opportunity that had excited the founders of the colonies was
to a very great extent counteracted by a strong countervailing
force: an inability—common to Europeans and American alike—
to define the present except in terms of the past. In this situation,
the Anglo-American colonies came increasingly to be thought of
not as new societies that would fulfill dreams people had been
unable to realize in Europe but as a field for ambition and a place
of opportunity for individuals and as valuable adjuncts to the
economic and strategic power of Britain.[32]

III

Although it can be argued that throughout much of the early modern era the vast unexplored and unorganized spaces of America were of enormous significance in helping to excite and to sustain Europe's dreams of making a new beginning for mankind, it cannot be suggested that in the early eighteenth century America provided much immediate inspiration for the Enlightenment. Indeed, when Enlightenment philosophers wanted to point to an example of an enlightened society, they turned to England itself, not to England's American colonies or to any other part of America, which remained largely "peripheral to Europe's experience of itself." But this situation changed radically after Britain's long, drawn-out, and intense quarrel with its American colonies beginning in 1765 had first focused attention upon them and then driven them to revolt and independent nationhood. As these Anglo-Americans first defiantly stood up for their rights and then sought to transform themselves into an extensive new republic with a government created by themselves on enlightened principles, exponents of the Enlightenment both in Britain and on the Continent examined the state of Anglo-American society more thoroughly and found it to be a close approximation, in many ways, an almost perfect demonstration, of their dream of a new order "in which men would escape from poverty, injustice, and corruption and dwell together in universal" prosperity, virtue, "liberty, equality, and fraternity."

Having long been valued for the gold, silver, sugar, tobacco, and rice that it sent back to enrich the old world, America, specifically British North America as it was reorganized into the new United States, now came to be celebrated because it seemed to represent an "immediate [and working] application of most of the controversial social and political ideas [then] under discussion in Europe." As such, America suddenly became "an example to the world," in the words of Turgot, "the hope of the human race," living, heartening proof that men had a capacity for growth, that reason and humanity could become governing rather than merely critical principles," and that, in the manner of Plato's Republic, philosophers of the kind who produced the Declaration of Independence, the new republican state constitutions, and the Federal Constitution of 1787, could become governors. "Who could not experience a thrill of pleasure," exclaimed the Marquis du Chastellux ecstatically, "in thinking that an area of more than a hundred thousand square leagues is now being peopled under the auspices of liberty and reason, by men who," free from the corrupting vices and luxuries of the old world and from the restraints of the dead hand of the past, made "equality the principle of their conduct and [simple] agriculture the principle of their economy?"[33]

As the United States came to be celebrated as a "laboratory for Enlightenment ideas" and the "workshop for liberty" by Europeans, it acquired the respect not only of the outside world but also of its own people. For virtually the entire existence of the British-American colonies, their inhabitants had measured themselves against metropolitan England and found themselves wanting. Now in view of their heroic achievements during the last quarter of the eighteenth century, they learned, to paraphrase a contemporary remark of Thomas Paine, that they had long thought better of the European world than it deserved. No longer did Europe seem to be the center of the world. Now, instead of Americans going to school to Europe, Europe was going to school to America. As Americans thus came more and more, again in Paine's language, "to reverence themselves," Europe became, at least in the short run, the same sort of negative reference for them that they had earlier been for Europe, while those features of their society for which they had traditionally been so apologetic—its simplicity, its newness, its rusticity, its innocence, its very size and openness—suddenly came to be perceived not as deficiencies but as virtues, positive advantage that gave America a special place in the creation of a new, englightened order.

Some enthusiasts even revived the slumbering millennial hopes of the early Puritan settlers and once again touted America as the New Jerusalem and Americans as the chosen people. More common was the simple depiction of America as a seat of civic republicanism embued with the values of frugality, moderation, industry, and simplicity, the national home of peace, prosperity, justice, equality, freedom, and statemanship, an entity whose great Revolutionary heroes, exemplified in Charles Willson Peale's "Gallery of Great Men" in his museum in Philadelphia, showed that America—simple, undifferentiated America—was not merely a place of abundance and liberty but a scene for heroic actions, a theatre of fame. Given the glorious events of the 1770s and 1780s, who among Peale's contemporaries could doubt his optimistic and expansive prediction that in the future the Pennsylvania State House, now Independence Hall, would be "a building . . . more interesting in the history of the world, than any of the celebrated fabrics of Greece or Rome!"[34]

If America's accomplishments during the Revolutionary Era and the new appreciation of its social state helped, at least temporarily, to liberate it from its own sense of dependence and cultural inferiority, they also played a key role in enabling the whole Western world to free itself from the burden of the past by contributing to a transformation in social and political consciousness that was every bit as fundamental and far reaching as that produced in the religious sphere by the Reformation of the sixteenth and seventeenth centuries. As a result of this transformation, people came to be not only receptive but eager for change, to be oriented toward the present and future rather than the past, to be confident of the efficacy of human reason operating on—and generalizing from—experience to shape that present and future, and to be committed to the revolutionary hopes that the world might be changed for the better, that man might be liberated from the tyranny of his ancient prejudices, that what had formerly been perceived as manifest disorder in the autonomous behavior of free people might actually comprise the basis for a new kind of order, and that criteria for membership in the political nation should be universalistic rather than prescriptively narrow. Henceforth, instead of searching for Utopia in a remote corner of the world, instead of endeavoring to recreate some past golden age, men would create a wholly new world in the future—a world in which the inadequacies of past and present worlds would, as seemingly had already occurred in North America, at last be overcome.[35]

IV

That America had had a significant role in this important transformation has been the central thesis of this essay. Initially, in the sixteenth and seventeenth centuries, America had served as a place on which people in the Old World could project their hopes for recovering a lost world that had been simpler, better ordered, more benign, and more virtuous. Eventually, British North America, reconstituted as the United States, became a

concrete example that encouraged people to project their hopes
for a better world into the future. No matter that the new American Republic had to some degree deceived the Old World, that, to
a major extent, the liberty, prosperity, and expansiveness it provided for so many of its free inhabitants had been and for another
seventy-five years would continue to be purchased at the cost of
keeping a large part of its population in chains, that American
culture continued to be in so many respects crude, provincial, and
derivative, or that Americans themselves turned out to be more
devoted to the pursuit of material self-interest than to the cultiva-
tion of that republican virtue they had appeared to epitomize at
various points during their Revolution. By seeming to provide a
harbinger of the future progress to which mankind could aspire,
America in the late eighteenth century had helped Europe finally to transcend its ancient obsession with the past and had
nourished on both sides of the Atlantic the confident and widely
diffused expectation that the future would become mankind's
most valuable inheritance.

Notes

1. Peter Gay, "The Enlightenment," in C. Vann Woodward, ed., *The Comparative Approach to American History* (New York, 1968), 38; Donald H. Meyer, *The Democratic Enlightenment* (New York, 1976), viii, xiii–xvii, xix.

2. Gay, "Enlightenment," 34, 38, 40; Meyer, *Democratic Enlightenment*; Henry F. May, *The Enlightenment in America* (New York, 1976).

3. J. H. Elliott, *The Old World and the New, 1492–1650* (Cambridge, 1970), 2–3, 56–59; Margaret T. Hodgen, *Early Anthropology in the Sixteenth and Seventeenth Centuries* (Philadelphia, 1964), 113; Michael T. Ryan, "Assimilating New Worlds in the Sixteenth and Seventeenth Centuries," *Comparative Studies in Society and History* 23 (1981): 519. For similar views, see also G. V. Scammel, "The New Worlds and Europe in the Sixteenth Century," *Historical Journal* 12 (1989): 389–412, and *The World Encompassed: The First European Maritime Empires c. 800–1650* (Berkeley and Los Angeles, 1881); and Elliott, "Renaissance Europe and America: A Blunted Impact?," in Fredi Chiapelli, ed., *First Images of America: The Impact of the New World on the Old*, 2 vols. (Berkeley and Los Ageles, 1976), 1: 11–23. For contrary views, see Walter Prescott Webb, *The Great Frontier* (Austin, 1964); Ernest J. Burrus, "The Impact of New World Discovery Upon European Thought of Man," in J. Robert Nelson, ed., *No Man is Alien: Essays on the Unity of Mankind* (Leiden, 1971), 85–108; Arthur J. Slavin, "The American Principle from More to Locke," in Chiapelli, ed., *First Images of America*, 1: 139–64; and William Brandon, *New Worlds for Old: Reports from the New World and Their Effect on the Development of Social Thought in Europe, 1500–1800* (Athens, Ohio, 1986).

4. See, especially, Edmundo O'Gorman, *The Invention of America: An Inquiry into the Historical Nature of the New World and the Meaning of its History* (Bloomington, Ind., 1961), and Hugh Honour, *The European Vision of America* (Cleveland, 1975), 2.

5. Louis Le Roy, *Of the Interchangeable Course, or Variety of Things in the Whole World* (London, 1594), 127, as quoted by Ryan, "Assimilating New Worlds," 523; *The Essays of Montaigne*, trans. George B. Ives (Cambridge, Mass., 1925), 1: 171.

6. Henri Baudet, *Paradise on Earth: Some Thoughts on European Images of Non-European Man* (New Haven, Ct., 1965), 55; Elliott, "Renaissance Europe and America," 20; Loren Baritz, "The Idea of the West," *American Historical Review* 46 (1961): 617–40; Durand Echeverria, *Mirage in the West: A History of the French Image of American Society to 1815* (Princeton, 1957), vii. See also Harry Levin, *The Myth of the Golden Age in the Renaissance* (Bloomington, Ind., 1869).

7. Echeverria, *Mirage in the West*, viii; Frank E. and Fritzie P. Manuel, *Utopian Thought in the Western World* (Cambridge, Mass., 1979), 113; Sir Thomas More, "Utopia," in Henry Morley, ed., *Ideal Commonwealths* (London, 1901), 4; Bertrand de Jouvenal, "Utopia for Practical Purposes," in Frank E. Manuel, ed., *Utopias and Utopian Thought* (Boston, 1966), 219–20; Slavin, "American Principle," 146–47; Levin, *Myth of the Golden Age*, 92–93; Paul A. Jorgenson, "Shakespeare's Brave New World," in Chiapelli, ed., *First Images of America*, 1: 85–86; Brandon, *New Worlds for Old*, 8–11. J. H. Hexter, *More's Utopia: The Biography of an Idea* (Princeton, 1952), the most extensive and penetrating discussion of

More's tract, makes no mention of its relationship to the discovery of America.
8. See James A. Boon, "Comparative De-enlightment: Paradox and Limits in the History of Ethnology," *Daedalus* 119 (1980): 89.
9. Brandon, *New Worlds for Old*, 15, 143, 151, 165.
10. Several scholars have pointed out that Europe's traditional fixation on its own past had been intensified at the time of the discovery and exploration of America by its simultaneous recovery and glorification of antiquity and have emphasized the extent to which their conceptions of the New World were shaped by their new knowledge of the ancient world. See Scammel, "New Worlds and Europe," 393–96; Elliott, *Old World and the New*, 15–16; and Ryan, "Assimilating New Worlds," 526–34. See also Elliott, "Renaissance Europe and America," 20.
11. O'Gorman, *Invention of America*, 129–30; Elliott, *Old World and the New*, 26; Ryan, "Assimilating New Worlds," 520–21; Slavin, "American Principle," 146–47.
12. Howard Mumford Jones, *O Strange New World: American Culture, The Formative Years* (New York, 1964), 14–21, 35–36; Elliott, *Old World and the New*, 25–26; and "Renaissance Europe and America," 20; Slavin, "American Principle," 146–47; J. C. Davis, *Utopia and the Ideal Society: A Study of English Utopian Writing 1516–1700* (Cambridge, 1981), 20–23; Levin, *Myth of the Golden Age*, xv; More, "Utopia," 6; Francis Bacon, "New Atlantis," in Morley, ed., *Ideal Commonwealths;* Tommaso Campanella, "The City of the Sun," in *Ideal Commonwealths;* Frank E. Manuel, "Toward a Psychological History of Utopias," in Manuel, ed., *Utopias and Utopian Thought*, 70–80; Baudet, *Paradise on Earth*, 32.
13. Elliott, *Old World and the New*, 13–15, 26–27, 103, and "Renaissance Europe and America," 20; Jones, *O Strange New World*, 14–20; Antonello Gerbi, "The Earliest Accounts of the New World," in Chiappelli, ed., *First Images of America*, 1: 39; Baudet, *Paradise on Earth*, 31; Charles L. Sanford, *The Quest for Paradise: Europe and the American Moral Imagination* (Urbana, 1961), 75; Samuel Purchas, *Purchas His Pilgrims* (Glasgow, ed.), 1: 249, as cited by Scammell, "New Worlds and Europe," 409. See also, Anthony Pagden, *The Fall of Natural Man: The American Indian and the Origins of Comparative Ethnology* (Cambridge, 1982); Olive Patricia Dickason, *The Myth of the Savage and the Beginning of French Colonialism in the Americas* (Edmonton, 1984); Henry S. Bausum, "Edenic Images of the Western World: A Reappraisal," *South Atlantic Quarterly* 67 (1968): 672–87; and the various essays in Edward Dudley and Maximillian E. Novak, eds., *The Wild Man Within: An Image in Western Thought from the Renaissance to Romanticism* (Pittsburgh, 1972).

On a related theme, Ronald L. Meek, *Social Science & the Ignoble Savage* (Cambridge, 1976), analyzes the relationship between the perception of American Indians as living examples of a primitive state of society and the emergence of both a new interest in "natural" man among natural law theorists such as Grotious, Hobbes, Puffendorf, and Locke and, among eighteenth-century French and Scottish theorists, a new theory of the progressive development of society from rudeness to refinement "through four more or less distinct and consecutive stages, each corresponding to a different mode of subsistence, these stages being defined as hunting, pasturage, agriculture, and commerce." This four-stage theory, which held "that societies of the European type had normally *started out as and developed from* societies of the American type," of course also contributed to reinforce what Fulvio Papi has called "the presumptuous conceit of European civilization that in itself was realized the [highest development of the] nature of man." Papi, *Antropologiae Civita nel Pensiero de Giordano Bruno* (Firenze, 1968), 200; as quoted by Brandon, *New Worlds for Old*, 153. The quotations from Meek are from pages 2 and 40.

14. See, in this connection, Allen G. Debus, *Man and Nature in the Renaissance* (Cambridge, 1978), 1, 6–7, 116–21, 134–41; Charles Webster, *The Great Instauration: Science, Medicine and Reform, 1626–1660* (New York, 1976), 1–31.

15. On the rage for projects and its effects, see Joan Thirsk, *Economic Policy and Projects: The Development of a Consumer Society in Early Modern Europe* (Oxford, 1978). The expansion of trade and its effects may be followed in D. C. Coleman, *The Economy of England 1450–1750* (Oxford, 1977), 48–68, 131–50, and B. A. Holderness, *Pre-Industrial England: Economy and Society, 1500–1750* (London, 1976), 116–70, 197–220. See also Ralph Davis, *The Rise of the Atlantic Economies* (Ithaca, 1973), and Neil McKendrick and John Brewer, *The Birth of a Consumer Society: The Commercialization of Eighteenth-Century England* (Bloomington, 1982).

16. Baritz, "Idea of the West," 633; Levin, *Myth of the Golden Age*, 61; Jones, *O Strange New World*, 39–40, 57–61; Mircea Eliade, "Paradise and Utopia: Mythical Geography and Eschatology," in Manuel, ed., *Utopias and Utopian Thought*, 265–68; Honour, *European Vision of America*, 8; Elliott, *Old World and the New*, 80–81.

17. More, "Utopia," 6; Elliott, *Old World and the New*, 94–95; Jones, *O Strange New World*, 40–41; Hodgen, *Early Anthropology*, 361; Slavin, "American Principle," 146–47; Michael Kraus, *The Atlantic Civilization: Eighteenth-Century Origins* (Ithaca, 1949), 309; Brandon, *New Worlds for Old*, 44.

18. Norbert Elias, *The Civilizing Process: The History of Manners* (New York 1978).

19. See Keith Thomas, *Religion and the Decline of Magic* (New York, 1971).

20. See, in this connection, David Bevington, *Tudor Drama and Politics: A Critical Approach to Topical Meaning* (Cambridge, Mass., 1968); W. H. Greenleaf, *Order, Empiricism and Politics: Two Traditions of English Political Thought, 1500–1700* (Oxford, 1964); Webster, *Great Instauration*, 1–31; William M. Lamont, *Godly Rule: Politics and Religion, 1603–1660* (London, 1969); Gordon J. Schochet, *Patriarchalism in Political Thought: The Authoritarian Family and Political Speculation and Attitudes Especially in Seventeenth-Century England* (New York, 1975); James Daly, *Sir Robert Filmer and English Political Thought* (Toronto, 1979); C. B. McPherson, *The Political Theory of Possessive Individualism* (Oxford, 1962); Slavin, "American Principle," 152–59; Joyce Oldham Appleby, *Economic Thought and Ideology in Seventeenth-Century England* (Princeton, 1978); Isaac Kramnick, *Bolingbroke and His Circle: The Politics of Nostalgia in the Age of Walpole* (Cambridge, Mass., 1968); Eliade, "Paradise and Utopia," 261; Davis, *Utopia and the Ideal Society*, 86.

21. Ryan, "Assimilating New Worlds," 523; Hodgen, *Early Anthropology*, 114; J. H. Elliott, "Revolution and Continuity in Early Modern Europe," *Past & Present* no. 42 (1969), 43; Webster, *Great Instauration*, 1–31; Baudet, *Paradise on Earth*, 37–38; Levin, *Myth of the Golden Age*, 139–67; Robert Forster and Jack P. Greene, eds., *Preconditions of Revolution in Early Modern Europe* (Baltimore, 1970).

22. Magnus Morner, *The Political and Economic Activities of the Jesuits in the La Plata Region: The Hapsburg Era* (Stockholm, 1953); Silvio Zavala, "The American Utopia of the Sixteenth Century," *Huntington Library Quarterly* 10 (1947): 337–47, and *Sir Thomas More in New Spain* (London, 1955). See also, Scammel, "New Worlds and Europe," 397–98; Baudet *Paradise on Earth*, 37; Levin, *Myths of the Golden Age*, 93.

23. Echeverria, *Mirage in the West*, viii; Slavin, "American Principle," 139–49; John Locke, *Two Treatises of Government*, ed. Peter Laslet (New York, 1963), 343; Jorgenson, "Shakespeare's Brave New World," 85–86; Levin, *Myth of the Golden Age*, 61; Baudet, *Paradise on Earth*, 37.

24. Leo Marx, *The Machine in the Garden: Technology and the Pastoral Ideal in*

America (New York, 1964), 43–69; Levin, *Myth of the Golden Age*, 93,190.

25. Baritz, "Idea of the West," 634–37; Webster, *Great Instauration*, 44–45; Avihu Zakai, "Exile and Kingdom: Reformation, Separation, and the Millennial Quest in the Formation of Massachusetts and Its Relations with England, 1628–1660," Ph.D. dissertation, The Johns Hopkins University, 1982.

26. See the discussion of these early British-American social experiments in John M. Murrin, "Colonial Political Development," in Jack P. Greene and J. R. Pole, eds., *Colonial Anglo-America, 1607–1763* (Baltimore, 1983), 417–24.

27. Marx, *Machine in the Garden*, 62.

28. Murrin, "Colonial Political Development," 424. See also Lyman Tower Sargent, "Utopianism in Colonial America," *History of Political Thought*, (1983), 6:483–522.

29. See Richard Hofstadter, "America at 1750: A Social Portrait" (New York, 1971), 3–32; Kraus, *Atlantic Civilization*, 216–62; Jack P. Greene, "The American Colonies during the First Half of the Eighteenth Century," *Reviews in American History* 1 (1973), 69–75; Echeverria, *Mirage in the West*, vii–viii.

30. O'Gorman, *Invention of America*, 135–40; Elliott, *Old World and the New* 5; 50–51; Baudel, *Paradise on Earth*, 45; A. Bartlett Giamatti, "Primitivism and the Process of Civility in Spenser's *Faerie Queene*," in Chiapelli, ed., *First Images of America*, 1: 72–74; Marx, *Machine in the Garden*, 43–69; O. Mannoni, *Prospero and Caliban: The Psychology of Colonization* (New York, 1956); James Sutherland, "The Author of *Robinson Crusoe*," and Ian Watt, "*Robinson Crusoe*, Individualism and the Novel," in Frank H. Ellis, ed., *Twentieth Century Interpretations of Robinson Crusoe: A Collection of Critical Essays* (Englewood Cliffs, N.J., 1969), 25–54.

31. Echeverria, *Mirage in the West*, 3, 6, 14–19; Jack P. Greene, "Search for Identity: An Interpretation of Selected Patterns of Social Response in Eighteenth-Century America," *Journal of Social History* 3 (1970): 189–220; Henry Steele Commager, *The Empire of Reason: How Europe Imagined and America Realized the Enlightenment* (New York, 1977), 126–27; Meyer, *Democratic Enlightenment* xx–xxi.

32. See Kraus, *Atlantic Civilization*, 41–43; Hodgen, *Early Anthropology*, 189; Elliott, *Old World and the New*, 1, 102.

33. Kraus, *Atlantic Civilization*, 220; Echeverria, *Mirage in the West*, 3, 35, 38; Commager, *Empire of Reason*, 11–12; Gay, "Enlightenment," 36–37, 40–42; Honour, *European Vision of America*, 9–10; Ryan, "Assimilating New Worlds," 537.

34. Gay, "Enlightenment," 42; Meyer, *Democratic Enlightenment*, vii; Jack P. Greene, "Paine, America, and the 'Modernization' of Political Consciousness," *Political Science Quarterly* 93 (1978): 73–92; Samuel Williams, *The Natural and Civil History of Vermont*, 2 vols. (Walpole, N.H., 1794), 2: 310; Daniel J. Boorstin, "The Myth of an American Enlightenment," in *America and the Image of Europe: Reflections on American Thought* (New York, 1960), 19; Commager, *Empire of Reason*, 63–65; James West Davidson, *The Logic of Millennial Thought: Eighteenth-Century New England* (New Haven, 1977), 213–97; Edgar P. Richardson, Brooke Hindle, and Lillian B. Miller, *Charles Willson Peale and His World* (New York, 1982), 60, 92, 183.

35. Echeverria, *Mirage in the West*, 151–52; Elisabeth Hansot, *Perfection and Progress: Two Modes of Utopian Thought* (Cambridge, Mass., 1974), 95; Jouvenal, "Utopia for Practical Purposes," 220; Eliade, "Paradise and Utopia," 262–68.

The Constitution and the Citizen-Soldier

by

Allan R. Millett

Nations live on myths. No myth is more precious to a republic (whether it is democratic or socialist) than the notion of the people-in-arms springing to the defense of their homeland. Before the twentieth century the mythos of the "nation in arms" was shared at one time or another by such diverse states as Athens, Florence, Switzerland, France, and the United States. Fusing the Marxist-Leninist vision of the class struggle with the older tradition of popular defense, the Soviet Union, the People's Republic of China, Cuba, Nicaragua, and the Socialist Republic of Vietnam now provide additional testimony to the persistence of the concept of people's armies. The symbolism of the "nation in arms" transcends mere military functionalism. Instead it represents a fundamental judgment about the foundation of the state. As Thomas Jefferson put it: "The Greeks by their laws, and the Romans by the spirit of their people, took care to put into the hands of their rulers no such engine of oppression as a standing army. Their system was to make every man a soldier, and oblige him to repair to the standard of his country whenever that was reared. This made them invincible; and the same remedy will make us so."[1]

Jefferson describes all the elements of the militia ideal: (1) the history of republics showed that they remained republics only so long as they did not rely upon a standing army; and (2) the militia system required a universal military obligation, i.e., the right of the state to compel its male citizens to train and then to serve whenever they were called. These two elements of the militia myth, of course, contain inherent contradictions—or at the very least challenges of public policy of the highest order. The first assumption—that the militia will protect the Republic from praetorianism and tyranny—begged the question of whether the militia could meet other threats to a republic like foreign invasion or popular rebellion. (Who would watch the watchmen?) The questions of multiple military roles and missions, balanced against the principle of civilian control, bedeviled militia theorists and militia organizers, but discomfited the latter more than the former. The second assumption—that a democratic society could find the political will to compel military service, especially for peacetime training—proved equally knotty. The most awesome examples of the nation-at-arms (the phalanxes of Sparta and the impi of the Zulus) hardly reflected democratic values, although the pikemen of the Swiss cantons showed that military prowess and political liberty might not be incompatible.[2]

As they did in so many other ways, the Framers of the Constitution and the members of the first and second Congresses showed their ability to balance political idealism with a more pessimistic assessment of how men might really behave. Built on nearly two centuries of colonial experience, the Founding Fathers created a system of multiple institutions that met the varied tests they believed republicanism required. The system they created, designed principally to distribute military power between the federal government and the states and to further divide military power at the federal level between the President and Congress, would have to adjust to the military challenges the nation faced. The process of evolution has not been painless, and it has certainly been costly. From its birth in the colonial period, the concept of universal military obligation had mythic qualities, and the relative merit of standing and reserve forces has enriched the debate on defense policy throughout the Constitution's life.

The Militia Tradition of the Colonial Period

Although all the English North American colonies with the exception of Pennsylvania established the principle of universal military obligation and citizen-based defense, they also immediately modified these charters to limit their application. First, the obligation applied only to white, male citizens who were part of tax-paying, property-owning families, further modified by extensive occupational exemptions and age limitations. Second, the system was designed for training, not active service. The only real requirement was for militiamen to muster on some schedule, which might vary from one day a week to one day a quarter, so that the captain might check the accuracy of his roster, inspect equipment and arms (which the militiamen were supposed to furnish), and conduct rudimentary training in the individual soldierly skills and small unit tactics. In reality, the militia system in the colonies, as in England, was meant not only to allow some portions of the population to arm to support governmental authorities, but also to disarm the most discontented members of society, principally black slaves and freedmen, indentured servants, drifting manual laborers, and Indians and mixed-bloods. The positive benefits of the system were well understood. It allowed governors to appoint officers on a patronage basis, and it created a modest base of trained soldiers from which to draw the cadre of wartime forces, which were raised by some combination of volunteering and impressment.[3]

The actual use of enrolled militiamen against either the Indians or other European foes was rare and most often limited to local actions. Only in seventeenth-century tidewater Virginia and rock-rimmed New England did the militia function as it was conceived. Even then the colonists depended on professional soldiers for training (e.g., John Smith and Myles Standish), and when it came to leading provincial troops on extended operations, the colonials recruited professional officers whose ability and ruthlessness became legend: John Underhill, Benjamin Church, and Robert Rogers. Real war in North America—and there was plenty before 1775—had little to do with the militia. The militia might serve as a recruiting base, but it did not go to war in units. Within the statutory militia, one could, in addition, find volunteer units which set their own standards for membership, usually with governmental charter, but they did not go to war as units either. Instead, wartime provincial forces formed, served, and disappeared in accordance with the need of the moment. They might represent a reasonable cross-section of the militia—obligated population—as did William Pepperell's expedition to Louisbourg in 1745—or they might represent an attempt to rid the colonies of its male undesirables—as did the formation of Virginia Governor William Gooch's colonial battalions for the Cartagena expedition (1740–42). Even the French and Indian War, which produced the most extensive military

effort in the English colonies, did not alter the practice of forming
"war service only" battalions for expeditions either mounted independently or alongside British Army battalions. When Lt. Col.
George Washington marched for Fort Duquesne for the first
disaster of his illustrious military career, he marched at the head
of the 1st Virginia Regiment, an organization that bore no more
relationship to the Virginia militia than the Coldstream Guards.[4]

Throughout the colonial period, however, the English settlers
maintained the principle of universal military obligation and
citizen-based defense, whatever the military reality. Empirical
evidence had little to do with their insistence on principle. For
example, the statutory militia did not equip itself, either from
personal means or public funds. In the 1680s only 10 percent of
the Virginia militia had muskets, and the units of New England
and the Middle Atlantic states were no better armed. Only the
volunteer companies—armed social clubs—had enough weapons
for their members, and they were so small that they could hardly
contribute to any calculation of colonial military strength. The
militia's weakness was not regional. The Southern colonies
mounted periodic expeditions against the Indians and the Spanish and French posts in Florida and along the Gulf Coast. Invariably, they had to raise troops on an ad hoc basis, officers from the
gentry and "other ranks" from those portions of the population
that were excluded from militia membership. The patterns of
operations in wars against the French and Spanish garrisons in
North America revealed the militia's fundamental weakness. It
could not be used for operations that required troops to cross
colonial boundaries, and it could not be deployed as units beyond
limited compulsory periods of service. The militia might provide
local defense, but it was good for little else.[5]

The irony of the American Revolution is that it depended
upon a military system that had already proved bankrupt. The
situation in 1775 reflected a dispute that reached back to the turn
of the eighteenth century. After the Restoration, Charles II had
won control of the English militia in the Restoration Militia Statute (1661), an act that William of Orange embraced during the
Glorious Revolution. During the 1690s–1700s the English government attempted to bring militia reform to North America and
failed. After a complex series of maneuvers that originated from
London, the British government abandoned its scheme for colonial centralization that affected New England and the mid-

Atlantic colonies. The militia reform movement failed, largely because of the recalcitrance of the existing militia and the colonial assemblies, which insisted that the legislative branch—not the governors—had primacy in determining militia affairs. This interpretation was about fifty years behind English practice.[6]

The Revolution and the Constitution

At the same time the militia faded as part of the land forces of England it received a North American reprieve for its appearance—if not always performance—in the American Revolution. In the battles of 1775 Lexington, Concord, the British withdrawal to Boston, Bunker Hill—the New England militia demonstrated its ardor and skill in the tactical defense. In Virginia the Royal Governor, Lord Dunmore, found the militia an insurmountable barrier to control of the tidewater area. The same situation developed in North Carolina, ratified by the defeat of the Tory militia at Moore's Creek Bridge. So confident was the militia-based Whig army that it invaded Canada, only to come to ruin. The failure of the Canadian expedition was replicated by the defeat of Washington's mixed force in the campaign for New York City and northern New Jersey in 1776. Toward the end of that campaign, Washington delivered his judgment on the militia: "To place any dependence upon the militia is assuredly resting upon a broken staff."[7] The campaigns of 1776 and 1777 proved Washington's contention that the militia could not be depended upon to fight and vanquish English regulars. Until Saratoga and Monmouth, it was unproved that the Continental line could beat the British, either. In any event, the militia did not have to master the British infantry in eighteenth-century conventional battle to contribute to the Patriots' victory. Rather the militia battled the Indians and Tories along the Appalachian frontier, blunted Royal Navy raids from the sea, carried on partisan warfare against the British regulars and Tories in the Mid-Atlantic states and the South, and enforced the laws passed by the Whig assemblies. If one uses the same criteria applied by the Bolsheviks in Russia and the Communists in China, the Whig militia played an essential part in the revolutionary portion of the Revolution.[8]

The problem with the militia's performance was that it legitimized a military system that had already collapsed before the Revolution began. It appears as if the Whig militia—and its Tory counterpart—did truly represent the general population in ways that the Continental Army (at least its rank and file) did not. The militia system received an eleventh-hour reprieve when the victorious colonials adopted the Articles of Confederation in 1781 and in 1787 when they wrote the Constitution. Even the most ardent believers in regular troops—Washington, Greene, Knox, Hamilton, and von Steuben—accepted the political reality that the militia had survived the war. When the issue of the cost of standing forces (something in which the colonies had ample evidence) was joined with the dangers of centralized political control, the Federalists conceded that the nation's land forces would depend upon the militia for its major source of operational units. Their position, of course, was that the central government should have more influence on militia affairs. It was a position that defined the political struggles over control of the militia for the next 150 years.

The drafters of the Constitution argued over the status of the militia, but the issue was seldom in doubt. The Nationalists won a victory when Article I, Section 8, gave the Congress the power "to provide for calling forth the Militia to execute the Laws of the Union, suppress Insurrections and repel Invasions; To provide for organizing, arming, and disciplining the Militia, and for governing such Part of them as may be employed in the Service of the United States, reserving to the States respectively, the Appointment of the Officers, and the Authority of training the Militia according to the discipline prescribed by Congress." The President in Article II, Section 2, had the responsibility of commanding militiamen he called into federal service.[9]

The Antifederalists did not find the Constitution to their liking and mounted an effective opposition to ratification until the Federalists agreed to a "Bill of Rights" that would answer the Antifederalists' complaints. The militia clauses had a distinct Cromwellian odor about them—so the Antifederalists argued. The Constitution already implied that Congress had the lead in determining basic military policy. Now the Antifederalists wanted to secure the rights of the states to maintain military forces, even though the Constitution prohibited them from having standing armies and navies. As finally drafted and adopted, the Second Amendment to the Constitution reflected the value of civilian control and decentralized power, "A well regulated Militia, being necessary to the security of a free State, the right of the people to keep and bear Arms, shall not be infringed."[10] Since the Constitution and the Second Amendment gave both the federal government and the state governments responsibility for maintaining the militia, Congress attempted to define dual control in the Uniform Militia Act and Calling Forth Act in 1792 and subsequent legislation. The states passed their own statutes. The federal laws recognized the states' principal responsibility to organize and train the militia, but called for a uniform organization officered by the states. The senior state officer would be an adjutant general appointed by each governor. Congress rejected the Federalist proposal—advocated by Washington, Knox, and Hamilton—to create a "special corps" within the militia under direct federal control. Instead it gave the President the authority to call upon the states to provide militia for up to ninety days federal service. The President needed no special powers to repulse an invasion, but he found himself hedged by the requirements (variously defined over time) to receive calls for help from state governments and/or federal judges before acting against rebels or enforcing federal law with militiamen. As refined in 1795, federal law required militiamen to answer the President's call under the threat of fine and (for officers) cashiering, but only after trial by a court-martial of militia officers. The fines would be collected by a federal marshal.[11]

The compulsory aspects of the federal militia acts of 1792 appeared in even more pale form in the states' military laws. Although they echoed the principle of universal military obligation for white male citizens (ages 18–45), the state laws required only attendance at drill with nonattendance punishable by fines. If called to state duty, a militiaman could avoid service by commutation or by providing a substitute. State service was also bounded. States could not compel their militias to serve outside the home state, and the terms of service (although usually longer than the federal limit of ninety days) were not designed for extended duty. Although some states, particularly in New England, maintained armories and stored public weapons for militia use, the responsibility for arming and equipping still remained with the individual. The result was that the states were chronically short of weapons. The only armed, drilled, and equipped militia units were the volunteer companies, recognized in the federal legislation but essentially regulated by state statute. (The Uniform Militia Act actually gave the volunteer companies some protection, for "they shall retain their special privileges" even as they fulfilled the same obligations as the enrolled militia.) In all, the state systems gave the obligated militia, especially the well-to-do, ample opportunity to avoid any semblance of military duty. Money drove the system. Fines were irregularly collected, and the states had to pay the militia for state service at rates higher than federal military pay and competitive with civilian wage rates. The relaxed standards of the colonial period, thus, survived the throes of the Revolution and the early national period.[12]

From the passage of the Uniform Militia and Calling Forth Acts through the end of the War of 1812, the militia system had ample opportunity to demonstrate its strengths and weaknesses. As a force to repel invasion, the militia (if built on the volunteer companies and stiffened with regulars) proved effective against the British Army at Baltimore, Norfolk, Plattsburg, Sacketts Harbor, and New Orleans. Their performance along the Niagara frontier and at Bladensburg brought less glory. For extended operations the militia served only as short-term reinforcements for armies built around the regiments of the U.S. Army and state volunteers raised and led by regional military heroes like William Henry Harrison, Andrew Jackson, and Peter B. Porter. Enforcing federal law, the militia had an even more uncertain record. Mustered to quash the Whiskey Rebellion (1794) and Fries Rebellion (1798) and to enforce the Embargo Act of 1807, the militia proved difficult to assemble in a timely manner and too expensive for extended service. The American legal system erected further barriers to the use of the militia to enforce federal and state law, for American judges normally followed the English "Mansfield Doctrine" that soldiers serving under the direction of federal and state judges and law enforcement officers (marshals and sheriffs) did so as a *posse comitatus* of citizens, not as military men. This legal position meant that soldiers had no special protection from criminal and civil suits arising from their service as temporary police. The inherent legal problems of law enforcement only complicated the delicate federal-state political problems of using federal troops to "insure domestic tranquility."[13]

Aware that the states had not embraced their militia responsibilities with any great ardor, Congress attempted to prod the states toward militia reform with federal dollars as early as 1798. Concerned by chronic arms shortages among the federalized militia, Congress appropriated $400,000 for arms, which would be either sold to the states or stored under federal control for issue in a crisis. In 1803 Congress required the states to make an annual report of their militia strengths, organization, and stocks of arms and equipment. When Secretary of War Henry Dearborn finally collected the states' reports (albeit incomplete) in 1804, he concluded that the United States had over half a million enrolled militia, but that only 10 percent of these citizen-soldiers had weapons of their own. Four years later, in the middle of a war scare with Great Britain, Congress established an annual sum of $200,000 for the purchase of militia arms. The funds, however, would go only to those states that submitted annual reports that proved that they conducted musters and trained. The federal subsidy fell far short of the sum Dearborn estimated necessary to arm the militia, which was $50 million, and the money tended to go to those states (like New York and Massachusetts) that needed the money the least. In reality, only the volunteer companies armed and trained themselves with any constancy, subsidized by private patrons and small grants from the state and national governments.[14]

By the end of the Federalist and Jeffersonian period, an era in which the United States faced substantial peril from enemies foreign and domestic, the principles of universal military obligation and compulsory service had already eroded. The standing forces—the U.S. Army, U.S. Navy, and U.S. Marine Corps—depended upon volunteers to expand their ranks in wartime. The state volunteers attracted men away from the Army by better wages, less discipline, better promotion opportunities, and more limited terms of service. The two naval services competed for sailors and marines in the Atlantic Coast sea-faring communities, which meant that they lost recruits to the merchant marine and privateersmen in peace and war for much the same reasons the U.S. Army could not compete with the state volunteers. The statistics for the War of 1812 are illuminating. For the land forces, some 56,000 men served in the U.S. Army, 13,000 men in special federal volunteer units, and some 458,463 in state-raised units. (The latter figure is a bit misleading since it includes multiple enlistments for short terms of service.) The two naval services numbered roughly 12,000 officers and men in 1814, while the privateering force (some five hundred vessels sailed with letters of marque and reprisal) must have been at least twice as large. Moreover, all of the American land and naval forces shared common missions, except perhaps ship engagements on the high seas. Coast and harbor defense, for example, involved in practice whatever forces were available with militiamen manning gunboats and sailors and marines fighting ashore. The concept of phased degrees of mobilization readiness for especially trained and equipped forces did not take root for another century.[15]

The Militia in the Nineteenth Century, 1815–1898

During what C. Vann Woodward has called "the century of free security," the United States depended upon the state militias for wartime reserves, while at the same time national authorities avoided using federalized state forces for law enforcement purposes with the notable exception of 1861–1865. For lesser challenges to federal authority than the Civil War, like the Nullification Crisis of 1830 or the Pullman Strike of 1894, Presidents preferred regular troops, whose use caused fewer political and managerial problems. On paper the states fulfilled their duties. As new states joined the Union, they obediently passed militia laws to conform with the Act of 1792 as amended. In reality, compulsory militia service disappeared by the Civil War. Under pressure from all sorts of lobbies, the states abolished required musters and drills after eliminating fines for nonattendance. At the front of the militia abolition movement were church-based peace societies, workingmen's associations, and loose coalitions of rural and urban politicians whose constituents had tired of paying commutation fees and fines—or in some cases providing free labor on public roads in lieu of militia service. Only the volunteer companies kept the concept of the citizen-soldier alive long enough to lay the foundations of the modern National Guard.[16]

In two national mobilizations the volunteer companies—sometimes organized into cohesive regiments in the Eastern states—provided the first wave of volunteers raised to fight the Mexican and Civil Wars. In Ohio, for example, militiamen provided three regiments of volunteer infantry in 1846. In the spring of 1861 2,000 militiamen rallied to form the first two regiments of volunteer infantry raised by the state of Ohio and sent to Washington in time for the first Battle of Bull Run. North and South, the experience was the same as volunteer units, many of them newly formed, entered wartime service. Two famous regiments of the city of New York—the 7th Regiment and the

69th Regiment—illustrate two patterns. The 7th New York retained its militia status and served two short federal tours during the war; its ranks, however, provided 600 officers to the Union Army. The 69th New York, formed by Irish patriots to train for a war against England, volunteered intact for the Union Army, much to the relief of local politicians and Catholic prelates who found it a disruptive force in city politics.[17]

By the War with Spain (1898), the volunteer militia regiments, which by now largely called themselves the National Guard, offered to field more troops than the War Department wanted. Pressured by guardsman constituents, the McKinley administration and Congress increased the call for volunteers from 60,000 to 125,000 (there were then 114,000 volunteer militiamen according to War Department records) and gave the existing Guard regiments the first chance to enter federal service with their unit identity intact and their own officers in command. Again, Ohio's experience is illustrative. In the 1890s the Ohio Guard numbered between 5,000 to 6,000 and spent about $100,000 a year, three-quarters of it state funds. Even before the call for troops on April 25, 1898, the Ohio Guard had recruited its strength up to almost 9,000 men and soon thereafter reached its limit of 10,000 men in eight infantry regiments, one separate infantry battalion, a cavalry regiment, and four artillery batteries. Of the 551 officers who entered federal service, only about 100 were not prewar Guard officers, and the majority of the new officers were Guard NCOs. In the infantry regiments only one-quarter of the enlisted men had no military service. In addition, the state built and supplied a mobilization camp in Columbus that provided far better facilities than the guardsmen found when they fell under War Department control. The mobilization in every state but Kansas followed the same pattern: prewar Guard regiments provided the organizational skeleton and most of the muscle for the state volunteers mustered into the Volunteer Army in 1898.[18]

The War with Spain also demonstrated that the volunteer reserve movement had spread to the naval services. Led by Massachusetts in 1890, fifteen states had organized small naval militia units for coast and lakes defense; in 1898 the naval militia numbered around 4,500 officers and men. Almost to a man the naval militia volunteered for wartime service in the U.S. Navy. The concept of employment for the naval militia differed from that of the National Guard, for the naval militia and the Navy Department agreed that the wartime citizen-sailors should serve as individual fillers, not as crews. Although six auxiliary cruisers carried crews composed largely of naval militiamen, the majority of the volunteers served on regular crews. Impressed by the potential of the naval militia, the Navy Department soon proposed both a federal naval reserve (eventually created in 1916) and a degree of federal control (including the obligation of wartime service) over the states' naval militia, a goal achieved in 1914.[19]

The mobilization of 1898 heartened National Guard reformers, most notably those Guard officers who had founded the National Rifle Association (1871) and the National Guard Association (1879), but it also did little to dampen the Guard's critics, most notably officers of the U.S. Army. On the plus side, the National Guard of 1898 was a far more stable and effective military organization than it had been at its rebirth in the 1870s. The Guard regiments in the Pullman Strike of 1894 showed a higher level of discipline and competence than their performance in the Railway Strike of 1877. State support for the Guard had climbed to $2.3 million by 1891, and another militia act in 1887 had increased the annual federal subsidy to $400,000. Nevertheless, following the scathing indictment of Bvt. Maj. Gen. (Colonel, U.S. Army) Emory Upton in his unpublished and incomplete *Military Policy of the United States*, officers of the Regular Army had developed a long list of familiar complaints about the Guard. The Army's conventional wisdom—reflected by its own Uptonian mobilization plan of 1898—was that the National Guard could not be sufficiently reformed to serve as a reliable wartime reserve force.[20]

The Army's critique focused on the institutional weaknesses linked with dual control, sanctioned by the Second Amendment and the subsequent militia acts passed by Congress. The list of Guard flaws was comprehensive and in part accurate:

a. Guard officers did not meet federal standards in military education and depended upon political influence and unit popularity for their commissions. Senior officers, including the state adjutant generals' staffs, were especially unfit.

b. Guardsmen insisted on federalization by unit and continued unit integrity after federalization, which only prevented the optimal use of guardsmen's military skills and the perpetuation of slack command and persistent indiscipline. Experienced soldiers from the Guard should be distributed throughout a wartime Army, not remain concentrated in hometown units.

c. Guard units might train individual soldiers, but they could not train as units, even at the company level. They were too small, did not have adequate equipment and training facilities, did not attend weekly drills or the five-day summer camp in adequate numbers or for a long enough period of time, and had no one present who could set Regular Army standards.

d. State duties, especially riot control and disaster relief, detracted from training for wartime operations.

e. The state governments would not provide funds for adequate armories, training sites, and mobilization camps.

f. Guardsmen, especially the older officers and NCOs, were not physically fit for field service, and Guard medical officers were not sufficiently rigorous either when guardsmen enlisted or when guardsmen mustered into federal service. Emergency medical examinations upon mobilization took too much time and caused too much unit turnover at a time when personnel stability was essential.

Although individual Army officers had served amicably as Guard advisers since the late 1880s and several hundred of them had served with the Army's blessing as Volunteer officers in 1898, the War Department's official position in 1899 was that the Second Amendment prevented significant reform of the National Guard. Instead, the Army wanted Congress to assert its constitutional right under Article I, Section 8, to create a reserve force that would be under complete federal control.[21]

Reform of the National Guard and Creation of the Reserves

At the height of the Progressive Era the United States reformed its military mobilization system, in the process creating a new constitutional relationship between the federal government and the states. Like many other reforms of the Progressive Era, the national interest emerged dominant, but not completely so. But from 1900 until 1916, the War and Navy Departments assumed the principal responsibility for creating and supporting land and naval reserve forces. In the constitutional sense, Article I, Section 8, took precedence over the Second Amendment, but it did so only because the political context for defense policy had changed. First, the United States after 1898 had assumed responsibility for the defense of territories, commonwealths, and protectorates beyond the North American continent. In addition, it had entered a period of international rivalry with the great powers of Europe and the Japanese Empire, which in theory could send invasion fleets to the Western Hemisphere—or at least establish bases and colonies in Mexico and the Caribbean basin. Last, Americans seemed prepared to let the national government collect taxes and finance public projects that in the past had been reserved to private enterprise or state initiative. In a narrower sense, the attentive public wanted Congress to bring more rationalism and efficiency to military affairs, which meant more planning for mobilization and more influence by professional officers on defense matters. After a century of independence and aggressive insistence upon its political uniqueness, the United States was ready to follow European examples in shaping its military institutions.[22]

Congress demonstrated its interest in militia reform in 1900 by increasing the annual subsidy to $1 million, and in 1902 it held hearings on a War Department bill, endorsed by the National Guard Association, to replace the Uniform Militia Act of 1792. The idea of milita reform received support from influential congressmen (including Congressman Charles Dick of Ohio, a committee chairman and National Guard major general), Secretary of War Elihu Root, President Theodore Roosevelt, and a significant portion of the Army officer corps. All the reformers agreed that the organized militia, i.e., the volunteer National Guard, might become the Army's first source of wartime reinforcements if fueled with federal dollars and supervised by the War Department. The National Guard leadership did not rally uniformly behind this change of emphasis upon mission, for the general pattern of state subsidies for the Guard had been on the increase. The source of state interest, however, was the Guard's utility in suppressing labor disputes (also on the rise), a mission many guardsmen did not relish. The Guard lobby, however, found obnoxious provisions in the War Department's 1902 draft legislation. The central offending provision was an article that allowed the federal government to create a reserve force unconnected with the militia provisions of the Constitution. This provision allowed the Army to recruit soldiers, then discharge them as veterans into a pool of obligated reserves much like the British

Army system then in effect. When Congress passed the Militia Act of 1903, the provision for a federal reserve force had disappeared from the legislation. Another casualty of the compromise bill (known as the Dick Act) was the suggestion that the government might raise federal volunteers before it turned to the Guard for wartime reserves. The Guard wanted to be the first reserves called—but on its terms.[23]

The Militia Acts of 1903 and 1908 linked the National Guard to the U.S. Army in ways considered visionary in the 1890s. The Guard accepted substantial obligations: to drill twenty-four times a year, which meant one night every two weeks, to attend a one-week summer camp, and to train at drill and summer camp in accordance with U.S. Army regulations and performance standards. Federal subsidies, which jumped to $2 million (1903) and then $4 million (1908), would go only to organized units that accepted federal attendance standards; a complicated subsidy system rewarded those Guard units that trained most with the Regular Army. Federal funds could be used not only to purchase arms and equipment but to pay guardsmen to train. In return, the War Department became obligated to accept all Guard units (regardless of arm) upon mobilization before it asked for federal volunteers. The War Department, however, did not have to maintain Guard units in their original form upon mobilization, but the Guard accepted this potential risk since most Guard units were infantry and expected to serve as such. In addition, the Guard would be represented within the War Department by a Division of Militia Affairs, which would report directly to the Secretary of War, not to the War Department General Staff (1903), which guardsmen distrusted. The 1908 act provided the most sweeping change upon the Guard's post-mobilization service: once accepted as federal troops the Guard could serve for a period of time determined by the federal government and beyond the limits of the continental United States.[24]

On the surface the Militia Acts of 1903 and 1908 represented a new status for the Guard. In complementary actions Secretary Root opened Army schools to Guard officers, assigned Regular officers as permanent advisers to those Guard units that requested them, and authorized more joint Army-Guard maneuvers. Federal subsidies to the Guard soon reached a 1:2 ratio to state contributions. The War Department took seriously its obligation to supply the most modern arms and equipment to the

Guard. Between 1903 and 1916 the federal government spent $53 million on the Guard, more than its total expenditures between 1872 and 1903. In 1912, however, the Justice Department and the War Department—in a fit of constitutional legalism—took the bloom off the reform movement by issuing an opinion that the militia still drew its essential legitimacy from the Second Amendment, which meant that the National Guard, even if it volunteered for federal service as units, could not be deployed outside the continental United States. This interpretation of the law, unchallenged in the courts, brought the militia reform movement to a temporary halt since the War Department General Staff needed troops for overseas reinforcements, not continental defense.[25]

The National Guard soon found itself challenged by a War Department effort, championed by Maj. Gen. Leonard Wood, chief of the General Staff (1910–1914), to create a reserve force outside the organized militia. In the end the National Guard prevailed, largely because of its influence in Congress, but its victory was incomplete. In another round of military reform in 1915–1916 the Guard defeated a War Department proposal to create a federal reserve force (the visionary "continental army" plan), but it did so only by accepting substantial modifications to its status as the first land force reinforcements in wartime. In exchange for more federal control (forty-eight drills) and a dual enlistment oath, which obligated guardsmen for federal service and federal standards upon enlistment, the Guard maintained its position that it should be the principal source of *units* for wartime service. The national government would provide more funds for training, including drill pay.

The National Defense Act of 1916, however, provided the foundation for a separate federal reserve force built around a pool of officers unattached to the militia system. As students of military mobilization from George Washington to Leonard Wood had concluded, the central defect the United States faced was not finding able enlistedmen, but the serious shortage of junior officers. The War Department had already found alternative sources: college students who had taken military training in the land-grant colleges established by the Morrill Act of 1862, citizen volunteers who had participated in Army-sponsored summer camps (the "Plattsburg Movement") begun in 1913, and civilian professionals whose skills might be used by the Army as specialist-officers upon mobilization. Although the National Defense Act of 1916 further legitimized the National Guard as the source of prewartime trained units, it opened the door for development of another reserve force by authorizing the Army's Officers Reserve Corps. This precedent was further reinforced by a complementary movement to give the Navy Department the ultimate control over the states' naval militias (and their marine detachments) in legislation passed by Congress in 1914–1918. In sum, the reserve reform movement of the Progressive Era had provided the War and Navy Departments the congressional sanction to develop reserve forces programs that did not depend upon state cooperation. Although the most extreme version of reserve forces reform—the concept of compulsory peacetime military training—went down to resounding defeat in the "Preparedness Movement," the national government had clearly established its right to establish the conditions under which it would accept reserve forces into federal service in wartime.[26]

The Constitution and the Reserve Forces in the Era of World War and Cold War

The constitutional compromise reflected in the National Defense Act of 1916 on the authority to raise reserve forces has now survived more than seventy years, four major wars, two lesser federal mobilizations (1916 and 1961), and thousands of natural disasters and civil disturbances. It has also passed from volunteerism through conscription and back again to volunteerism. The compromise is at once ingenious and illogical. The national government may use its authority under Article I, Section 8, to create reserve forces, even those that drew their original legitimacy from the Second Amendment and the state militia tradition. Even though the federal government determined the National Guard's primary mission preparing units for active military service in times of crisis—and provides virtually all of the funds that support the Guard, it did not prohibit the states from using the Guard for state missions. At the same time the Guard could not use its influence in Congress to prevent the creation of a separate Army Reserve and Air Force Reserve, but it could insist upon the creation of the greatest anomaly of all, an Air Force National Guard. The naval services, on the other hand, severed their connection with the naval militias and developed reserve forces

with no constitutional ambiguity and no special roots outside
their parent services.

The nationalization of the Guard accelerated after World War
I when Congress in 1920 amended the National Defense Act of
1916. Another set of amendments in 1933 removed the last
constitutional ambiguities, if not the last conflict between the
Army and the Guard over the execution of reserve policy. Although all land forces before 1940 recruited volunteers, the legislation of the period had to assume that another war would bring
conscription as it had done in 1917, an assumption that complicated Army-Guard relations. In addition, the Guard had to accept that Congress would authorize the War Department to build
a federal reserve force with no constitutional ties to the Second
Amendment. The 1920 legislation provided the basic concept:
that the three major components of the land forces constituted
one army, the Army of the United States. In wartime volunteers
and conscripts would enter the Army of the United States
through the Regular Army, the National Guard, and the Organized Reserve. Congress again rejected proposals for compulsory
peacetime military training, which reflected public attitudes in
the 1920s and 1930s. It did, however, eliminate the last vestiges
of uncertainty over the status of the National Guard in 1933 by
declaring that federally recognized and supported militia units
now constituted "the National Guard of the United States of
America," an organic component of the Army of the United
States that the President might mobilize when Congress declared
a state of national emergency. The Guard could be federalized for
periods determined by the national government and sent anywhere in the world, as some guardsmen learned to their dismay
in 1941 and 1942.[27]

The legislation of 1920 and 1931 recognized that the National
Guard would train in peacetime and fight in wartime as tactical
units, up to and including full divisions, as it had in World War I.
The legislation, however, did not bring simplicity to the Army's
reserve components because of its provisions for training peacetime reserve officers. World War I had again demonstrated a
critical Army weakness, small unit leadership. The 1920 legislation repeated and strengthened the 1916 concept of an Officers
Reserve Corps; Guard officers could henceforth hold rank in the
Officers Reserve Corps and escape federal screening upon mobilization. What concerned Guard leaders was that the ORC,

which manned the headquarters cadre of Army Reserve divisions, would attract quality volunteers in such numbers that the Guard could not improve its own leadership. The rank structure in the Officers Reserve Corps provided exciting chances for advancement since it reflected a force structure of a minimum of six divisions. In 1939 the National Guard numbered almost 200,000 members, but the Officers Reserve Corps ran a close second with 116,000 members. The Guard, however, held a substantial advantage since it paid its members to drill, and the ORC did not. Throughout the 1930s, for example, the Army provided only about one-quarter of the ORC with paid active duty training and limited that training to one two-week period. When pressed to fund training and provide equipment for its reserve components, the War Department favored the Guard as the Congress intended. Ironically, the Army Reserves of the interwar period soon voiced the same complaints about the Guard that the Guard had made about the Regular Army before World War I.[28]

The last great test of federal-state relations occurred during the disorders that arose during the rise of the civil rights movement in the 1950s and the subsequent urban race riots and antiwar campus disturbances of the 1965–1970 period. In every test of presidential authority to use troops, especially those of the National Guard, Presidents Eisenhower, Kennedy, Johnson, and Nixon won in the courts and in Congress. The use of troops in civil disturbances, however, also revealed that the public would criticize the whole Army when the Guard, sometimes operating under state military laws that did not conform to Department of the Army regulations, demonstrated little competence for riot duty. At the Kent State killings of May 1970, for example, Ohio Army National Guardsmen were not bound by the same strict rules on the use of deadly force then applicable to the U.S. Army. Defense Department pressure, however, soon brought Guard riot control doctrine into conformity with federal standards. The riots of the period also demonstrated that the state governors still might require military forces, for in 1965–1971 guardsmen participated 261 different times in civil disturbances. In Ohio, for example, guardsmen saw duty during these years in thirteen natural disasters, six prison riots, and twenty-seven civil disturbances. Even though the Guard depended on federal dollars and trained for mobilization, it remained available for state functions as the Second Amendment intended.[29]

If one portion of the fundamental constitutional struggle over reserve forces policy had largely been resolved before the United States entered World War II, another set of conflicts and accommodations emerged after the war. As the question of dual federal-state control of the Guard sank under the accumulated weight of federal dollars, the demands of a national security policy based on deterrence and forward, collective defense produced a new set of issues, some of which were simply old issues recast in Cold War terms. Although reserve policy conflict eludes easy simplification, the fundamental battle lines are now drawn betwen the shared responsibility of the President and Congress to "provide for the common defense." Presidents, principally through the Department of Defense, have emphasized policies designed to man and equip the active duty forces, while Congress, responding to its reserve forces constituents rather than the nation's military professionals and DOD civilians, has viewed the reserve forces with more sympathy. Of course, the National Guard Association of the United States remains the most effective reserve forces lobby, followed by the Reserve Officers Association. Only one President, Dwight D. Eisenhower, sought reserve forces reform and then probably for the wrong reasons, the cost-savings he anticipated by a major reduction in the active forces' conventional war capability. Perhaps Secretaries of Defense Robert S. McNamara and Melvin Laird should be counted as champions of the reserve forces, but their vision of reserve forces improvement stemmed from fiscal and political problems rooted in their active duty force programs.[30]

At issue are basic differences over the likelihood that the United States will ever fight a protracted conventional war that will require a full mobilization of its reserve forces. During the Korean War the federal government called only one-quarter (about 600,000 of 2.5 million) of its obligated reservists to active duty; only one-third of the Army National Guard entered federal service. The Air Guard and Air Force Reserve called around 150,000 men to active service, which represented about 80 percent of the Air Guard and much of the new Air Force Reserve. More Army reservists (about 250,000) served than Army guardsmen (138,000) since the Department of the Army determined that it needed to bring its existing units to wartime strength and to provide experienced replacements to its divisions in Korea. The 1968 mobilization was even more limited; about 37,000 guardsmen and reservists from the Army, Air Force, and Navy entered active service.[31]

The emphasis upon the readiness of the active duty forces produced the nation's first extended experiment with obligated peacetime military service, for between 1948 and 1973 Congress provided the Department of Defense with the authority to take conscripts through the Selective Service System. The wars in Korea and Vietnam, of course, had a great deal to do with the survival of the draft, but the threat of the draft in 1953–1965 stimulated volunteer enlistments in the "all-volunteer" Air Force, Navy, and Marine Corps while the Army actually took draftees to make up for its shortage of volunteers. Congress attempted to provide some order to the concept of obligated service, active duty, and service in the reserve components in a series of laws that began with the Universal Military Service and Training Act of 1951 and continued through the Reserve Forces Acts of 1952 and 1955. Although the legislation never cured the equity problems (exposure to combat and the inconvenience of extended active duty) that had emerged with a vengeance during the Korean War, this additional flurry of reserve forces reform did bring change. The laws eventually allowed a potential draftee to enlist directly into a reserve component and thus exchange a two-year service obligation in the Army (and longer in the other services) for a much shorter period of initial active duty training (six months in the Army, Air Force, and Marine Corps, but two years in the Navy), followed by seven and a half years in the reserves. The laws further provided that most of the reserve service had to occur in organized units and that the individual reservist had to attend all scheduled training or face involuntary recall to active duty. Although the Army Guard objected to some provisions of the two Reserve Forces Acts, e.g., control of recruit training, it had to accept its having to conform or lose federal funds.[32]

The last major test of wills between the Department of Defense and Congress occurred in 1966 and 1967 over the issue of reserve components reorganization and produced the Reserve Force Bill of Rights and Revitalization Act of 1967. Although Congress accepted that the Secretary of Defense could control the allocation of reservists between the Selected Ready Reserve (drill-pay units) and the Individual Ready Reserve (individuals obligated to serve but not in a drill-pay status) and could control each service's plans to abolish, create, or redesignate reserve units, it asserted its ultimate right to use the legislative process, principally the annual task of defense authorization and appropriation, to make binding decisions upon reserve force structure, modernization, manning, and personnel policies. Although Congress has now provided the President with the authority to call 200,000 reservists to active duty without special congressional authorization, the War Powers Act of 1973 binds the President in his use of reserves just as it binds his use of active duty forces. There is little question that Congress, asserting its constitutional authority from Article I, will ensure that the current "Total Force" Policy will reflect its judgments, not just those of the Department of Defense.

The reserve components of the American armed forces have become neither Washington's "broken staff" nor Peter B. Porter's "shield of the republic," judgments accurate enough in their own way in their own time. The active duty forces outnumber the trained and ready reserves (2.2 million to 1.6 million), and only the Army's reserves are larger in numbers than the Regular forces (1.05 million to 781,000). At the same time all four armed services annually testify that they cannot—and will not—fight another conventional war without using reserve units for augmentation and reinforcement and calling to duty Individual Ready Reserves to bring active units up to war strength. As it has in other aspects of America's public life, the Constitution has proved both durable and elastic in providing reserve forces.[33] This responsibility, however, has produced a continuing series of Constitutional struggles for domination of the policy process. The current suit filed by the state of Minnesota to challenge the constitutionality of the Montgomery Amendment to the Defense Authorization Act Fiscal Year 1987 should come as no surprise. If nothing else, it proves that the memory of the militia tradition has persisted as a symbol of the federal system. Certainly the founding fathers' fears of praetorianism have faded. Their concern that the nation would paralyze itself with internal political controversy are not so easily dismissed. If continued vigilance is the price of liberty, so too is intelligence and moderation in providing for the common defense. At issue is the federal government's authority to send Guard units to "dangerous" foreign locations for annual training duty.

Notes

1. Quoted in Robert D. Heinl, ed., *Dictionary of Military and Naval Quotations* (Annapolis, Md.: Naval Institute Press, 1966), 192.

2. For the political ideology in Anglo-American militia tradition, see especially Lois G. Schwoerer, *"No Standing Armies:" The Antiarmy Ideology of Seventeenth Century England* (Baltimore, Md.: Johns Hopkins University Press, 1974) and John K. Rowl, "Origins of the Second Amendment: The Creation of the Constitutional Rights of Militia and of Keeping and Bearing Arms," Ph.D. dissertation, Ohio State University, 1978.

For the general history of the militia and National Guard, I have relied principally upon John K. Mahon, *History of the Militia and the National Guard* (New York: Macmillan, 1983); Jim Dan Hill, *The Minute Man in War and Peace* (Harrisburg, Pa.: Stackpole Company, 1964); and Elbridge Colby, *The National Guard of the United States* (Manhattan, Kans.: Military Affairs/Aerospace Historian Publishing, 1977). On American civil-military relations, see Allan R. Millett, *The American Political System and Civilian Control of the Military: An Historical Perspective* (Columbus, Ohio: Mershon Center, Ohio State University, 1979) and Allan R. Millett and Peter Maslowski, *For the Common Defense: The Military History of the United States of America* (New York: Free Press, 1984).

I also profited from reading a short study from the U.S. Army's Strategic Studies Institute: Maj. Samuel J. Newland, "The Militia's Role in National Defense: A Historical Perspective," ACN 87005, 15 May 1987, in the author's possession.

For bibliographical publications on Guard and Reserve policies and organization, see Headquarters, Department of the Army, *Civilian in Peace, Soldier in War: A Bibliographic Survey of the Army and Air National Guard* (Washington, D.C.: Department of the Army, 1967); Office of the Assistant Secretary of Defense (Manpower and Reserve Affairs), *The Guard and Reserve in the Total Force* (Washington, D.C.: Department of Defense, March 1974); and John K. Mahon, "Bibliographic Essay on Research into the History of the Militia and the National Guard," *Military Affairs* 48 (April, 1984): 74–77.

3. For differing perspectives on the colonial militia, see especially Daniel J. Boorstin, *The Americans: The Colonial Experience* (New York: Random House, 1958), 345–72; John Shy, "A New Look at Colonial Militia," *William and Mary Quarterly* 20 (April, 1963): 175–85; and Douglas Leach, *Arms for Empire: A Military History of the British Colonies in North America, 1607–1763* (New York: Macmillan, 1973), 1–41. for an assessment of the literature on colonial military history, see E. Wayne Carp, "Early American Military History," *The Virginia Magazine of History and Biography* 94 (July 1986): 259–84.

4. Leach, Arms for Empire, 42–79, 206–61, 307–50.

5. For important studies of the colonial militia, see William L. Shea, *The Virginia Militia in the Seventeenth Century* (Baton Rouge, La.: Louisiana State University Press, 1983); Darrett B. Ruttman, *A Militant New World, 1607–1640* (New York: Arno, 1979); John E. Ferling, *A Wilderness of Miseries* (Westport, Ct.: Greenwood Press, 1980); Fred Anderson, *A People's Army: Massachusetts Soldiers and Society in the Seven Years' War* (Chapel Hill: University of North Carolina Press, 1984);

Larry E. Ivers, *British Drums on the Southern Frontier: The Military Colonization of Georgia, 1733–1749* (Chapel Hill: University of North Carolina Press, 1974); Stewart L. Gates, "The Militia in Connecticut Public Life, 1660–1860," Ph.D. dissertation, University of Connecticut, 1975; David W. Cole. "Organization and Administration of the South Carolina Militia System, 1670–1783," Ph.D. dissertation, University of South Carolina, 1948; Richard H. Marcus, "The Militia of Colonial Connecticut, 1639–1775," Ph.D. dissertation, University of Colorado, 1965; Theodore H. Jabbs, "The South Carolina Colonial Militia, 1633–1733," Ph.D. dissertation, University of North Carolina, 1973; Archibald Hanna, "New England Military Institutions, 1693–1750," Ph.D. dissertation, Yale University, 1951; Jack S. Radabaugh, "*The Militia of Colonial Massachusetts*," *Military Affairs* 18 (Spring, 1954): 1–18; Louis Morton, "The Origins of American Military Policy," *Military Affairs* 22 (Spring, 1958): 75–82; and E. Milton Wheeler, "Development and Organization of the North Carolina Militia," *North Carolina Historical Review* 41 (July 1984): 307–23.

6. Rowland, "Origins of the Second Amendment," 216–52.

7. Washington's unhappiness about the militia is expressed in two letters to the Continental Congress, 24 September and 20 December 1776 in John C. Fitzpatrick, ed., *The Writings of George Washington*, 39 volumes (Washington, D.C.: Government Printing Office, 1931–1944), 5:110, 403.

8. For one recent assessment, see Allan R. Millett, "Whatever Became of the Militia in the History of the American Revolution?" George Rogers Clark Memorial Lecture, 24 October 1986, to be published by the Society of the Cincinnati, Washington, D.C.

9. Constitution of the United States (1787–1789), Article I, Section 8, and Article II, Section 2. For detailed analysis, see especially Richard H. Kohn, *The Eagle and the Sword: The Federalists and the Creation of the Military Establishment in America, 1783–1802* (New York: Free Press, 1975) and Rowland, "Origins of the Second Amendment," 351–414.

10. Amendment II, Constitution of the United States (1787).

11. "Militia," in H. L. Scott, comp., *Military Dictionary*, originally printed in 1861 (reprint, Westport, Ct.: Greenwood Press, 1968), 419–24.

12. Mahon, *History of the Militia and National Guard*, 46–77; John K. Mahon, *The American Militia: Decade of Decision, 1789–1800*, University of Florida Monographs, Social Sciences no. 6 (Gainesville, Fla.: University of Florida Press, 1960) and Lawrence D. Cress, *Citizens in Arms: The Army and Militia in American Society until the War of 1812* (Chapel Hill: University of North Carolina Press, 1982)

13. For the War of 1812, see Harry L. Coles, *The War of 1812* (Chicago: University of Chicago Press, 1965). On the use of federal and state forces in civil disturbances, see the essays in Robin Higham, ed., *Bayonets in the Streets* (Lawrence: University Press of Kansas, 1969) and David E. Engdahl, "Soldiers, Riots, and Revolution: The Law and History of Military Troops in Civil Disorders," *Iowa Law Review* 57 (October, 1971): 1–73. See also Robert Reinders, "Militia and Public Order in Nineteenth-Century America," *Journal of American Studies* 2 (April, 1977), 81–101, and Martin K. Gordon, "The Militia of the District of Columbia, 1790–1815," Ph.D. dissertation, George Washington University, 1975.

14. Mahon, *History of the Militia and National Guard*, 63–77.

15. Marvin A. Kreidberg and Merton G. Henry, *History of the Military Mobilization of the United States Army, 1775–1945* (Washington, D.C.: Department of the Army, 1955), 24–60; Charles O. Paullin, *History of Naval Administration, 1775–1911* (Annapolis, Md.: Naval Institute Press, 1968), 119–58.

16. Mahon, *History of the Militia and the National Guard*, 78–124. For an excellent

description of the antebellum period, see Marcus Cunliffe, *Soldiers and Civilians: The Martial Spirit in America, 1775–1865* (Boston: Little, Brown, 1968).

17. Among the best studies of the state organized militia in the nineteenth century, see William Packer Clarke, *Official History of the Militia and National Guard of the State of Pennsylvania*, 3 vols. (Philadelphia: J.C. Handler, 1909–1912); Emmons Clark, *History of the Seventh Regiment of New York*, 2 vols. (New York: The 7th Regiment, 1890); John Nankivell, *History of the Militia Organization of the State of Colorado, 1860–1935* (Denver: W. H. Kistler, 1935); Staff of the Cleveland Plain Dealer, *Official History of the Ohio National Guard and Ohio Volunteers* (Cleveland, Ohio: Plain Dealer Publishing, 1901); Joseph J. Holmes, "The National Guard of Pennsylvania: Policemen of Industry, 1865–1905," Ph.D. dissertation, University of Connecticut, 1970; Richard G. Stone, Jr., *A Brittle Sword: The Kentucky Militia, 1776–1912* (Lexington: University Press of Kentucky, 1977); Kenneth R. Bailey, "A Search for Identity: The West Virginia National Guard, 1877–1921," Ph.D. dissertation, Ohio State University, 1976; George C. Bittle, "The Organized Florida Militia from 1821 to 1920," Ph.D. dissertation, Florida State University, 1965; Jerry M. Cooper, "To Be a Soldier: History of the Wisconsin National Guard in the Nineteenth Century," unpublished manuscript, 1976; Patrick H. McLatchy, "The Development of the National Guard of Washington as an Instrument of Social Control, 1854–1916," Ph.D. dissertation, University of Washington, 1973; Patrick D. O'Flaherty, "History of the 69th Regiment, New York State Militia, 1852–1861," Ph.D. dissertation, Fordham University, 1963; John G. Westover, "Evolution of the Missouri National Guard, 1804–1919," Ph.D. dissertation, University of Missouri, 1948; Brian D. Fowles, "A History of the Kansas National Guard, 1854–1975," Ph.D. dissertation, Kansas State University, 1982; Matt Oyos, "The Mobilization of the Ohio Militia in the Civil War," seminar paper, Ohio State University, June, 1987; Don L. Lair, "To See the Elephant: Mobilization of the Ohio Militia in 1846," seminar paper, Ohio State University, June, 1987.

18. On the national mobilization for the War with Spain, see Graham A. Cosmas, *An Army for Empire: The United States Army in the Spanish-American War* (Columbia, Mo.: University of Missouri Press, 1971), 5–8, 69–110; David F. Trask, *The War with Spain in 1898* (New York: Macmillan, 1981), 145–77; and Kreidberg and Henry, *History of Military Mobilization in the United States Army*, 141–73. For Ohio I have relied upon Adjutant General, State of Ohio, *Annual Report of the Adjutant General to the Governor of the State of Ohio . . . 1898* (Columbus, Ohio: Westbote, Co., 1899).

19. Harold T. Wiand, "History of the Development of the United States Naval Reserve, 1889–1941," Ph.D. dissertation, University of Pittsburgh, 1952; Hill, *Minute Man in Peace and War*, 139–49.

20. For the issue of the militia reform, see especially William H. Riker, *Soldiers of the States: The Role of the National Guard in American Democracy* (Washington, D.C.: Public Affairs Press, 1958); Russell F. Weigley, *Towards an American Army* (New York: Columbia University Press, 1962) 100–161, and Colby, *The National Guard of the United States*, Ch. 2. On the question of the use of troops in labor disturbances, see Jerry M. Cooper, *The Army and Civil Disorder: Federal Military Intervention in Labor Disputes, 1877–1900* (Westport, Ct.: Greenwood Press, 1980). For one state's experience, see Brian Linn, "Pretty Scaly Times: The Ohio National Guard and the Railroad Strike of 1877," *Ohio History* 94 (Summer–Autumn, 1985): 171–81, and Charles A. Peckham, "The Ohio National Guard and Its Police Duties, 1894," *Ohio History* 83 (Winter, 1974): 51–67.

21. Maj. Gen. William H. Carter, "The Organized Militia," in his *The American Army* (Indianapolis, Ind.: Bobbs-Merrill, 1915), 267–94, summarized the devel-

opment of the antimilitia opinion in the Army. As a member of The Adjutant General's Office, Carter was intimately involved with militia affairs for more than twenty years.

22. For the changes in military policy in the Progressive Era, see James L. Abrahamson, *America Arms for a New Century: The Making of a Great Military Power* (New York: Free Press, 1981) and Richard D. Challener, *Admirals, Generals, and American Foreign Policy, 1898–1914* (Princeton, N.J.: Princeton University Press, 1973).

23. The most detailed analysis of militia reform is Louis Cantor, "The Creation of the Modern National Guard: The Dick Militia Act of 1903," Ph.D. dissertation, Duke University, 1963, which actually covers the period 1877 through 1916. See also Mahon, *History of the Militia and National Guard* 138–53, and Colby, *National Guard of the United States*, Chs. 2 and 3.

24. Cantor, "The Creation of the Modern National Guard," 165–262.

25. Colby, *National Guard of the United States*, Ch. 4.

26. Kreidberg and Henry, *History of Mobilization of the United States Army*, 175–213; Colby, *National Guard of the United States*, Ch. 6. See also John P. Finnegan, *Against the Spector of the Dragon: The Campaign for American Preparedness, 1914–1917* (Westport, Ct.: Greenwood Press, 1974) and John G. Clifford, *The Citizen Soldiers: The Plattsburg Training Camp Movement, 1913–1920* (University Press of Kentucky, 1972). On the reserve forces of the Navy Department, see Wiand, "History of the Development of the United States Naval Reserve," previously cited, and Public Affairs Unit 4–1, *The Marine Corps Reserve: A History* (Washington, D.C.: Division of Reserve, HQMC, 1966).

27. Colby, *National Guard of the United States*, Chs. 8 and 9. For atypical state experience in the interwar period, see Robert L. Daugherty, "The Ohio National Guard, 1919–1940, Ph.D. dissertation, Ohio State University, 1974.

28. Richard B. Crossland and James T. Currie, *Twice the Citizen: A History of the United States Army Reserve, 1908–1983* (Washington, D.C.: Office of the Chief, Army Reserve, 1984), 33–54.

29. In addition to Higham "Bayonets in the Streets" previously cited, see Robert W. Coakley, Paul J. Scheips and Vincent H. Demma, *Use of Troops in Civil Disturbances Since World War II, 1945–1965*, Office of the Chief of Military History Study 75, rev. ed. (Washington, D.C.: Department of the Army, 1971) with Supplements I and II (1971 and 1974), which cover the period through 1967. For the Ohio Guard's experience, see Paul H. Herbert, "Where There is Tumult: The Ohio Army National Guard and Civil Disturbance Control, 1965–1970,: A.M. thesis, Ohio State University, 1982. The statistics on Ohio are from the author's "Ohio National Guard Selected Chronology, 1861–1978." On the legal context, see especially Clinton Rossiter, *The Supreme Court and the Commander-in-Chief*, rev. ed. (Ithaca, N.Y.: Cornell University Press, 1976), 196–208.

30. For postwar reserve policy, see George W. Sinks, "Reserve Policy for the Nuclear Age: The Development of Post-War American Reserve Policy, 1943–1955," Ph.D. dissertation, Ohio State University, 1985, as well as the other books on reserve forces already cited. On reserve forces political skills, see Martha Derthick, *The National Guard in Politics* (Cambridge, Mass.: Harvard University Press, 1965); Martha Derthick, "Militia Lobby in the Missile Age—The Politics of the National Guard" in Samuel P. Huntington, ed., *Changing Patterns of Military Politics* (New York: Free Press, 1962), 190–234; and William F. Vantrosser, *Congress and the Citizen-Soldier* (Columbus, Ohio: Ohio State University Press, 1967).

31. For a review of postwar reserve policy, see Herman Boland, "A Historical

Survey of U. S. Reserve Forces Policy," Study 2, Part IV, *Studies Prepared for the President's Commission* (Gates Commission) *On an All Volunteer Armed Force* (Washington, D.C.: Government Printing Office, 1972). Although I have consulted the statistics in the Boland study for the Korean and Vietnam wars, they must be used with caution since they include active duty personnel conveniently designated as "reserves" who were not prewar and obligated reservists. See also Mahon, *History of the Militia and National Guard*, 208–11; Crossland and Currie, *History of the United States Army Reserves*, 95–100; and Charles J. Gross, *Prelude to the Total Force: The Air National Guard, 1943–1969* (Washington, D.C.: Office of Air Force History, 1985), 58–89.

32. Crossland and Currie, *History of the United States Army Reserve*, 100–102, 120–24.

33. Office of the Secretary of Defense, *Annual Report of the Reserve Forces Policy Board Fiscal Year 1986* (Washington, D.C.: Department of Defense, 1987). See also Bennie J. Wilson III, ed., *The Guard and Reserve in the Total Force* (Washington, D.C.: National Defense University, 1985).

A Question of Sovereignty:
The Militia in Anglo-American
Constitutional Debate 1641–1827

by

Lawrence Delbert Cress

The militia—a force consisting of citizen-soldiers for whom the bearing of arms is not a primary occupation—holds a special place in the constitutional and military history of the early American Republic. Inheritors of the classical republican suspicion of professional soldiers, Americans debated the merits of a citizen-soldier long after most nations, including Great Britain, had accepted the Regular Army as the best means to guarantee external security and domestic tranquility. Despite the citizen-soldier's mixed record during the Revolutionary War, few Americans could imagine a republican form of government without a militia. If not military prowess, the militia symbolized sovereignty, the ultimate source of power in society. Thus, access to and control of the citizen-soldier was a constitutional matter of high priority within the states, at the national level, and between the state and federal governments throughout the late eighteenth and early nineteenth centuries.

This essay explores the assumptions behind, and implications of, the militia powers granted the national government in 1787 by examining English precedent and American practice. Many of the ideas that shaped American thinking about the militia's constitutional importance had roots in seventeenth-century English constitutional debates. Tensions arising from competing royal and parliamentary claims for control over the militia contributed to the fall of Charles I and continued to influence English constitutional thinking through the Glorious Revolution. Revolutionary Era American state constitutions mirrored many older English concerns about executive tyranny. They also provide a context for understanding Federalist-Antifederalist differences over the militia that emerged during the ratification of the Constitution. Finally, the debate over the militia during the War of 1812 sheds light on the evolution of the federal system of government during the early national period.

English Precedent

The effort to control and direct the military capacity of armed citizens in England dates back to a late-thirteenth-century statute prohibiting the nobility from coming armed to parliaments and other assemblies called by the king.[1] Fifty years later, the Statute of Northampton threatened Englishmen with the forfeiture of their armor and imprisonment for confronting the king's justices and ministers "with force of arms" or for riding armed through markets and fairs.[2] The statute was little regarded, however. In 1383 and again in 1396 Richard II signed new laws limiting the bearing of arms "without the king's special license" in an effort to prevent conduct "contrary to the form of the statute of Northampton."[3]

These statutes were more concerned with maintaining public order than marshaling military might. Nevertheless, they suggest something of the armed citizen's place in early English society. First, the tranquility of the realm took precedence over the inclinations of armed individuals; public display of "dangerous and unusual weapons" was prohibited. Equally important, bearing arms was a social privilege, not a constitutional right. These statutes did not prohibit the wearing of arms appropriate to an individual's rank and standing. Respectable persons were expected to be prepared "to suppress dangerous riders, rebels, or enemies . . . of the realm"[4]—the same duties outlined for militiamen in federal service in the Constitution of the United States.

Medieval and early modern English militia law paralleled the statutes governing the private use of arms. Henry II's Assize of Arms (1181) and Edward I's Statute of Winchester (1285) linked specific military obligations to income and social standing. Similarly, Henry VIII required all subjects receiving lands, honors, offices, and other "hereditaments" from the king to bear arms in the "defense of the realm, or against his rebels and enemies."[5] The feudal assumptions behind these laws had largely disappeared by the late sixteenth century, but the link between military responsibility and socioeconomic status remained. Under Elizabeth I peers served as militia lord lieutenants, commanding county units composed of and financed by local aristocracy, members of the landed gentry, and well-to-do gentlemen. The stability of the realm dictated that local authority bend to the needs for the kingdom, however. Thus, the ultimate authority over these local units rested with the crown.[6]

Royal control of the militia and its well-to-do membership was an unquestioned assumption of English political life until the House of Commons claimed control of the militia for itself in 1641. The move immediately polarized the nation's political community, provoking civil war. At stake was far more than the control of the militia. Though far from a mighty military institution, it symbolized sovereignty. Without command of the militia, complained Charles I, "Kingly Power is but a shadow." The parliamentary leadership knew that, too. Their challenge was to offer a rationale for legislative rather than executive control of the nation's armed forces.[7] The arguments they offered are of interest to us because they echoed through the American debate over the militia during the early national period.

Charles I's claims were simple and straight forward. God and the law—beginning with the thirteenth-century statutes regulating the bearing of arms—gave the king the power to suppress rebellion and resist invasions. Thus, "no lawes [were] to be made, nor armes be taken up" without the king's consent.[8] Proponents of parliamentary power considered the king's position an affront to parliamentary prerogative and a claim to arbitrary power. Short on custom and legal precedent, though, they looked to necessity, reason, and natural law to support their claims.

Henry Parker, among the most influential of Parliament's advocates, understood that sovereignty was at the heart of the debate over the militia. While not a republican, he argued that princely power depended on popular trust. All "Power is originally inherent in the People," he wrote; "it is nothing else, but that might and vigor which . . . a societie of men containes in itself."[9] The king's authority over the militia, argued another essayist, dated to Parliament's request that Edward III appoint the high officers of the realm. Royal authority, then, was derived from the body politic, not God, and it was bound by laws enacted by Parliament. Hence, Parker and others, skipping over Parliament's own unrepresentative character, looked to that institution to ensure that the military power of the state served the common good. Parliament had, they claimed, an "inherent and underived authority" to protect itself and defend the realm.[10]

Other essayists were less certain of Parliament's prerogatives, though all concluded that existing circumstances justified the actions taken by the House of Commons. "In time of necessitie, illegal acts, are made legal: and things uterly against law, justifiable," wrote one supporter. Men gave their allegiance to the crown in exchange for protection under normal circumstances. But when the king failed to protect his subjects, that obligation fell to Parliament. To argue otherwise empowered the king to destroy the kingdom, while denying to the people the ability to defend themselves. In short, if the king failed to act in the interests of the realm, reason and necessity required that Parliament defend king and country. "The Parliament (which is the representative body of the Whole realme, and the eyes of all the kingdome) must of necessitie have the best cognizance and information of all imminent and approaching danger: ergo, they are the best and most competent judges of it."[11]

The conflict between Charles I and Parliament over the militia ended in civil war and the centralization of military power over the army and militia in the hands of Parliament. Some Englishmen, however, remained concerned. Parliament's power to raise an army, levy taxes for its support, and press men into service in and outside the kingdom exceeded that ever held by the crown. Should Parliament, any more than the crown, be entrusted with the power to raise both money and arms? asked an essayist advocating the decentralization of the militia in 1648. "The exercise of all which particulars are so many encroachments, or rather invasions upon the liberty and property of the subject," he concluded. Parliament's control of the militia only heightened concern. Under past practices, the king commanded the militia, but Parliament limited the uses to which it could be put. Neither "had power by law arbitrarily to exercise the militia after their own pleasures and wills."[12] The new arrangement, proponents of a strong local militia argued, opened the way for arbitrary government. At least for advocates of militia reform, the only sure defense against the misuse of military prerogatives was a strong militia founded in the counties.

Hope for a vital local militia structure disappeared with the purge of the House of Commons in December 1648. Cromwell's "Rump" Parliament preferred a standing army to the decentralized command structure envisioned by the Militia Ordinance of 1648. Indeed, in 1655 Cromwell transformed the nation's militia into an auxiliary of the professional army. Separated from the control of the local gentry, the militia was composed of paid volunteers and commanded by eleven major generals empowered to lead it into service anywhere in the realm. This new structure gave Cromwell a reliable military reserve able to suppress rebellion and crime, but it also enraged county gentlemen who resented being supervised or superseded by agents of the central government.[13]

The restoration of Charles II marked the end of Parliament's control of the militia. The militia acts passed in 1661, 1662, and 1663 returned command to the crown, made it unlawful to take up arms against the king or "those commissioned by him," and empowered lord lieutenants and their deputies to search and seize the weapons of any person deemed a threat to peace. Initially Charles used these expanded powers to disarm and imprison religious dissenters and to confiscate public arsenals in the towns they controlled. The old tension between local and centralized control of the militia remained, however, as the day-to-day control over the militia returned to the county gentry traditionally and ideologically suspicious of royal intrusion and interference. Indeed, the early efforts by the king and court to use the militia as an agent of centralized political authority failed in the face of determined local resistance led by lord lieutenants more loyal to their counties than the crown. Moreover, the Restoration Parliament, fearful of a powerful royal militia, would accept no militia that was not militarily innocuous, decentralized, and firmly under the control of the county gentry.[14]

Frustrated by his inability to remodel the militia after Cromwell's plan of 1655, Charles II turned to the Regular Army. The Disbanding Act of 1660 enabled the king to keep soldiers as long as he paid for them himself. Throughout his reign, Charles II maintained at his own expense a peacetime force of approximately 6,000 men. Parliament acquiesced, believing that a small army posed no threat so long as it controlled the kingdom's purse strings. Parliament even provided funds for an expanded army during the Dutch Wars of 1665–67 and 1672–74 and again in 1678 when war with France was expected, but it insisted that the army be reduced when each crisis passed.[15] The informal constitutional arrangement that kept peace between king and Parliament hardly survived the coronation of James II, however. The new monarch, using income newly granted by Parliament, expanded the size of the army, doubling the number of Catholic officers in the king's service and dispersing the army through the English countryside. In an effort to make the county militias more responsive to royal authority, James named Catholic officers to replace many Protestant lord lieutenants and deputies. Still suspicious that the locally oriented militia was unsuitable for furthering royal ambitions, James disarmed the militia in Ireland, Scotland, and in parts of England. Elsewhere, the militia ceased to train after 1685, often at the suggestion of the king. Only London's trained bands and the regiments of Dorset and Norfolk were capable of performing even local police duty by 1688. When William of Orange invaded, the militia was disorganized and disaffected, commanded by a mixture of inexperienced Catholics, often hated by those they commanded, and disillusioned Protestants unwilling to act on the king's behalf or ready to join the invading army of William of Orange.[16]

James II's use of the army and abuse of the militia contributed directly to his inglorious exile to France. According to Parliament, James had subverted Protestantism as well as the civil laws and liberties of the kingdom by "raising and keeping a standing army . . . without the consent of parliament" and by "causing several good subjects being Protestants to be disarmed, at the same time when papists were both armed and employed." The Declaration of Rights presented to William and Mary both redefined the military powers of the English king and restated long-standing assumptions about the armed citizen's place in the realm.

The revolutionary settlement prohibited the English monarchy from raising an army during peacetime without Parliament's consent. This changed fundamentally the crown's military prerogatives, tying the power to make war to the legislative authority of Parliament. The Declaration of Rights also guaranteed "that the subjects which are Protestants may have arms for their defence suitable to their conditions, and as allowed by law." Though not explicitly a call for the revival of the militia, the assertion that every Protestant had a right to arms reaffirmed the value of the militia in the constitutional balance that guaranteed

English liberties. Implicit too was the notion that legitimate military power resided, not with an army created by the king and/or Parliament, but in the independent citizenry composing the county-based militia units. Finally, by consciously making access to arms subject to legislative enactment and social rank, the revolutionary settlement continued the ancient custom of giving men the right to possess arms according to their social and economic standing, except that Catholics were now denied that privilege. Considering the prevailing legislation restricting the ownership of guns to persons holding property with a "clear yearly value of 100 pounds per annum," this effectively limited the right to bear arms to the Protestant upper class.[17]

As it happened, the new constitutional arrangement helped render moot the debate between king and Parliament over the militia. Parliament, as always suspicious of the royal influence in the counties, had no interest in promoting a strong militia system. A revived militia, even if membership were limited to the Protestant upper class, would only enhance the king's independence from Parliament. The House of Commons, at least, entered the reign of William III convinced that its new fiscal power over the Regular Army offered the best avenue by which to control the crown's military ambitions. The crown, on the other hand, had little interest in devoting its resources to rebuilding county militias best known for their undependability. Besides, the military demands that came with a war with France on the Continent required the steady and reliable service of trained regulars. By the first decade of the eighteenth century, only the Old Whigs, intellectual heirs of the republican theorists of the mid-seventeenth century, remained convinced that a vital militia offered the only sure means of preserving liberty and national security. These political thinkers doubted Parliament's ability to act on its military powers independent of royal influence.

American Revolutionary Constitutions

In America some eighty years later, the militia while not renowned for its exploits in the field was still a military and civil institution to be reckoned with. Like the members of Parliament in 1688, delegates to state constitutional conventions during the Revolutionary Era wrote constitutions with an eye toward ensuring that their government's military capacities did not become the vehicle for executive tyranny. While every state named the governor the commander in chief of both militia and regular state troops, the real power to mobilize the states' military institutions belonged to the representative assemblies. Regular troops could not be raised or officers commissioned in any state without the consent of the elected assembly, and in some states the right of the governor personally to lead the state's troops was circumscribed. Most states also limited the civilian appointments an active duty military officer could accept. The purpose was to ensure that military commissions were not used to expand the power and influence of the governors or to undermine the autonomy of the state assemblies.[18] Neither were state governors given unlimited control over their respective militias. Only in Massachusetts did the governor hold an independent power to call out the militia. There the people gave the governor broad military powers, but retained a popularly elected militia officer corps. Most states required the consent of an executive council (usually chosen by the general assembly) before the militia could be mobilized. Moreover, state constitutional conventions largely denied governors a role in the appointment of militia officers, preferring to divide that power between the militia's rank and file and the representative assembly. Virginia and New York were the only exceptions: the former required the governor to consider the recommendations of the county courts and the latter made gubernatorial appointments dependent on the advice of the executive council.

The Articles of Confederation exhibited the same concern about the centralization of military authority. The Continental government had the authority to raise (with the consent of nine states) an army, direct its operation, establish rules for its conduct, and appoint general and staff officers under its control. Nevertheless, the states controlled the means by which the troops were to be mobilized, and they appointed officers through the regimental level. The Continental government had no control over or access to the states' militia forces. The state delegations that met in Philadelphia during the summer of 1787 dramatically changed the locus of military power in the new republic. The new Constitution granted Congress the power to declare war and to raise, support, and regulate an army and navy. Congress also was given the power to organize, arm, and discipline the militia and the authority to call it out to enforce federal laws, maintain civil order, and expel foreign invaders. Command over all troops raised for federal service, whether regular or militia, was vested in the office of the President. Except in emergencies the states were prohibited from raising troops without congressional consent.

Still, constitutional safeguards rooted in the political theory of seventeenth-century England prevented the misuse of the military arm of government. Congress could raise and support armies in peacetime, but appropriations were limited to two-year terms. The powers to raise and command troops also were divided between the legislative and executive branches. Federal access to the state militias was limited, too. Congress could call out the militia, but only to enforce federal law, suppress insurrections, or repel invasions. Finally, the states retained supervisory authority over congressionally prescribed militia training programs as well as the right to appoint militia officers.[19]

The Constitution's military provisions generated a heated debate over the implications of centralized military power, however. Antifederalists feared the reordering of the Republic's military powers principally because they doubted the national government's ability to reflect popular sentiment. Republican government, they thought, worked in the states because the people were regularly in touch with their representatives. Delegates to Congress would represent districts many times larger than those of state assemblymen. Their terms of service would be longer too, further reducing contact with their constituents. To give a governmental body incapable of representing the public interest the power to raise armies and to organize and call out the militia was tantamount to granting a king sole control over the military forces of his realm. The Antifederalists feared that, like the English kings of the Restoration, the proposed federal government would saddle the young Republic with an oppressive and expensive standing army.

Antifederalists were equally concerned that the state militias would suffer under the new constitutional order. Opponents of the Constitution knew only too well that ambitious monarchs, like Charles II and James II, had deprived citizens of their liberties by raising standing armies while neglecting the militia. To give an unrepresentative Congress control over the arming, training, and organizing of the citizen militia opened the way for a similar scenario in the United States. Luther Martin reminded Marylanders that "When a government wishes to deprive its citizens of freedom, and reduce them to slavery, it generally . . . leaves the militia in a situation as contemptible as possible." Congress, Martin contended, had the power "even to disarm" the militia.[20] Patrick Henry wondered whether "a single musket" would be left in the states after the Constitution went into effect.[21] Elbridge Gerry expressed similar concern two years later during the House debate over the Second Amendment, suggesting that only the feared "mal-administration of the Government" made an amendment guaranteeing arms for a "well regulated Militia" necessary.[22] Other Antifederalists suspected that the federal power to organize and discipline the militia would be used to harass and oppress the body politic. Citizens might be called out on long and arduous marches, or held in service indefinitely, all in an effort to compel the acceptance of Regular troops. Militia mobilization might also be used as a guise to place the population of an entire state under martial law. Talk of a select militia system composed of a fraction of eligible males generated concerns that the militia would be dominated by the young and propertyless—a force in every way but in name a standing army. In short, centralized control over the militia, no less than the Constitution's other military provisions, threatened the citizenry's ability to protect their republican liberties. Citizens inadequately represented in the councils of government and without the means to defend themselves faced the loss of republican institutions forever.

Federalists rejected the notion that effective representation required small electoral districts. A large electoral district, James Madison argued in *Federalist* No. 10, prevented the domination of special interests in the governmental process. It followed that if the state assemblies retained control over the Republic's military power the potential for abuse was far greater than if national representatives exercised that power. Moreover, Federalists were convinced that the division of military power held the potential for cataclysmic military competition between the states. The inability of the Continental government to respond to Shays' Rebellion had forced Massachusetts to raise its own army to put down the rebellion. Similar crises in the other states would transform the Confederation into thirteen disunited states perpetually on the brink of war. Alexander Hamilton argued that the smaller states, fearing attack by their stronger neighbors, "would endeavor to supply the inferiority of population and resources, by a more regular and effective system of defense, by disciplined troops and by fortifications." Other states would be forced to follow suit, making the federal-state balance embodied in the Articles meaningless. Neither would civil liberties fare well if interstate military rivalries developed. Since "it is the nature of war to increase the executive at the expense of the legislative authority," wrote Hamilton, the establishment of despotic rule in all the states would only be a matter of time.[23]

From the Federalist perspective, the failure to create a national military establishment would contribute to the proliferation of standing armies within the states and the destruction of civil liberties. The need for a dangerous standing army would disappear, however, if the national government could raise an army and mobilize the militia independent of the states. Protected by the sea from its enemies, the United States would require only a small body of troops to patrol the frontier, to protect the principal ports, and to guard the federal arsenals. The principal institution of national defense, except during extended hostilities, would be a nationally organized select militia.

Federalists dismissed charges that the militia under federal control would only be another name for a standing army. Citizen militia units, made up of the very people with the most to lose at the hands of a tyrant, were unlikely candidates for manipulation by ambitious politicians. On the contrary, a revitalized militia structure would create "a circumstance which increases the power and consequences of the people; and enables them to defend their rights and privileges against every invader."[24] Other Federalists argued that a national militia would necessitate only a small Regular Army while providing a check against their activities. Hamilton echoed the same sentiment in *Federalist* No. 29, concluding that a national militia establishment "appears to me the only security against it, if it should exist."[25] Thus the Federalist campaign for a national military establishment confronted the long-standing fear of a centralized military directly. Instead of undermining the principles of republican government, Federalists argued, the establishment of a militarily independent national government was essential for the survival of republican institutions in America.

All of this is not to say that the Federalists believed that a centralized military structure was incorruptible. Ambitious politicians could misuse any military organization. Federalists were confident, however, that the proposed Constitution contained every safeguard included in either the English Declaration of Rights or the American state constitutions. The power to raise armies resided in Congress, noted Madison, ensuring "that no armies shall be kept without legislative authority; that is without the consent of the community itself."[26] Biennial elections and the two-year limit on military appropriations further guaranteed that military legislation would be reviewed by representatives "fresh from the body of the people."[27]

If Congress abused its military prerogatives, the militia, Federalists were quick to point out, would always be available to protect the public interest. Far from eliminating the militia, the new Constitution promised to put it on a more respectable footing. Congress was charged with organizing and arming the militia—prerogatives that Federalists claimed could be exercised by the states if the national government failed to fulfill its responsibilities—while the states retained the authority to administer training and to appoint the militia officer corps. "Before a standing army can rule," argued Noah Webster, "the people must be disarmed," and that was unlikely as long as the states retained a hand in the training process.[28] Moreover, the federally organized militia structure itself promised to deter political tyranny. Second only to the constitutional and military importance of the armed citizenry, Madison contended, was "the existence of subordinate governments, to which the people are attached and by which the militia officers are appointed, [which form] a barrier against the enterprises of ambition, more insurmountable than any which a simple government of any form can admit of."[29]

The ratification of the new Constitution during 1787 and 1788 gave the national government total control over the republic's Regular forces. Americans continued to worry about the dangers inherent in the power to raise armies during peacetime, but few questioned the necessity of a centralized regular military establishment. The national government's power to organize, arm, and discipline the militia and to use it to enforce law, suppress insurrections, and repel invasions rested less easily in the national consciousness, however.

Numerous constitutional amendments urged by state ratification conventions underscore a lingering fear that the state militias were not adequately protected against abuses by the new central government.[30] The concern that the militia would be purposely neglected gave rise to proposals guaranteeing that the states could organize, arm, and discipline their citizens if Congress failed to fulfill its responsibilities. A more common fear, though, was that Congress' right to call out the militia would prove detrimental to republican liberties. New Yorkers recommended that the militia not be compelled to serve outside a state's borders longer than six weeks without legislative consent. Others worried that the subjection of the militia to martial law might lead to abuses. The Maryland convention believed that "all other provisions in favor of the rights of men would be vain and nugatory, if the power to subjecting all men, able to bear arms, to martial law at any moment should remain vested in Congress." Along with North Carolina, Maryland asked Congress to amend the Constitution so that the militia could be placed under martial law only "in time of war, invasion, or rebellion."[31]

Virginia's recommendations for constitutional revision are of particular interest because they directly shaped the militia guarantees included in the Bill of Rights. Declaring that "the people have a right to keep and bear arms," Virginians asked for constitutional recognition of the principle that "a well regulated militia, composed of the body of the people trained to arms, is the proper, natural and safe defense of a free state." That proposition addressed the fear that the new government, as had James II one hundred years before, would disarm the citizenry while raising an oppressive standing army. To reinforce the point, the Convention urged that the Constitution declare that standing armies "are dangerous to liberty, and therefore ought to be avoided, as far as the circumstances and protection of the community will admit."[32]

A year later, James Madison proposed to the House of Representatives that the Constitution be amended to provide that "The right of the people to keep and bear arms shall not be infringed; a well armed and well regulated militia being the best security of a free country." Responding to the widely held fear that Congress' access to the militia would be misused, the Virginia representative proposed that that amendment be placed alongside the other limitations on legislative power listed in Article I, Section 9, of the constitution. The congressional committee charged with preparing a slate of constitutional amendments, of which Madison was a member, recommended to the House a more explicit statement of the militia's importance to the constitutional order: "A well regulated militia, composed of the body of the people," the new language read, "being the best security of a free state, the right of the people to keep and bear arms shall not be infringed."[33]

The committee's recommendation raised few concerns in the House. The objections that surfaced sought only further to underscore the importance of the militia to republican government. Elbridge Gerry, for example, reminded the House that "Whenever Governments mean to invade the rights and liberties of the people, they always attempt to destroy the militia, in order to raise an army upon their ruins." Thus, he urged that the amendment be rephrased to require that the militia be "trained to arms." That language, he thought, would protect the militia from neglect by making it "the duty of the Government" to arm the citizenry for militia service. The motion died for lack of a second, though some congressmen remained convinced that stronger constitutional guarantees were necessary to prevent the abuse of Congress' prerogative to raise standing armies. To reenforce the principle that "a well regulated militia [was] the best security of a free state," South Carolina's Aedanus Burke proposed language declaring that a "standing army . . . in time of peace is dangerous to pubic liberty, and such shall not be raised . . . without the consent of two-thirds of the members present in both Houses." The House rejected that amendment too, but not because members disagreed with Burke's assessment of the dangers inherent in keeping a peacetime army. Objections focused on the parliamentary procedures involved in introducing the amendment and the requirement for a two-thirds majority for legislative action.[34]

Debate in the Senate followed a similar pattern. Senators defeated an amendment to insert "for the common defence"—apparently after "to bear arms"—while they agreed to rephrase the nature of the militia's relationship to the Republic's security, calling it "necessary to," rather than the "best" form of, national defense.[35] The first change no doubt reflected a desire to ensure that it was the militia that was to bear arms; its rejection reflected not the undesirability of that end but, rather, the feeling that the proposal was redundant. The decision to describe the militia as necessary to the national defense more accurately expressed the growing sentiment in the United States that in wartime Regular soldiers also had important roles to play in the defense of a republic.

A joint conference committee of the House and Senate accepted the Senate's revisions without debate and sent the militia amendment on to the states. As a statement of republican principle already commonplace in many state declarations of rights, it evoked little discussion. If objections were raised, and there is no evidence that they were, they probably centered on the amendment's failure to link the militia explicitly to the dangers represented by a standing army. Whatever the issues, "A well regulated Militia, being necessary to the security of a free State, the right of the people to keep and bear Arms, shall not be infringed" became part of the Constitution after Virginia ratified the Second Amendment in mid-December 1791. Henceforth, Congress was prohibited from taking any action that might disarm or otherwise render the state militias less effective.

The War of 1812

Despite the concerns that led to the drafting and ratification of the Second Amendment, the states had no occasion during the early national period to accuse the federal government of neglecting its obligation to arm, organize, and discipline the militia. To the contrary, the states proved reluctant to allow their militias to become instruments of the national defense, in the process raising constitutional questions about the command and control of the militia that remained unresolved into the antebellum period. Like the landed aristocracy of Restoration England, state and local officials jealously protected their local militia against the intrusion of national authority. Repeated attempts by Federalist and Republican officials at the national level to generate interest in a national militia structure received cool receptions by congressmen more interested in preserving local autonomy than in creating an effective national citizen militia—a circumstance not unlike that in England a century before.

The War of 1812 brought to a head constitutional differences between national and state authorities about the militia's place in the Republic's constitutional order that had festered for nearly twenty years. A look at the constitutional debate over federal control of and access to the militia that arose during the Republic's second war with Great Britain offers insights into the lingering debate over who should control the citizen-soldier.

In April 1812, Congress passed legislation assigning militia quotas to the states in the event of war. From the outset, the republican administration expected little cooperation from New

England's Federalist-dominated state governments. Indeed, even before the United States declared war on Great Britain, the lower house of the Massachusetts General Court had opened debate over whether the commonwealth should comply with a militia mobilization order from the federal government. When General Henry Dearborn, commander of the military district in New England, issued a call late in June for the New England governors to place part of their militia quota on duty for coastal and frontier defense, the governors of Rhode Island, Connecticut, and Massachusetts refused.[36] The constitutional debate that ensued focused on the prerogatives of sovereignty, raising basic questions about the ability of the national government to turn to the citizen-soldier for the defense of the Republic.

Massachusetts, Connecticut, and Rhode Island considered militia mobilization a state prerogative. While willing to organize its quota of militia soldiers, Rhode Island would allow its soldiers to take the field, its governor advised the War Department, only "when, *in my opinion*, any of the exigencies provided for by the constitution . . . under which they are detached, exists, agreeably to the opinion and advice of the council of this State, given me on the occasion."[37] Connecticut too initially expressed willingness to cooperate with federal military demands, assuming, of course, "that no demand would be made . . . but in strict conformity with the constitution and laws of the United States." When General Dearborn ordered five militia units to join federal forces stationed at New London and New Haven, however, state authorities raised constitutional objections. The Constitution, the governor's council noted, allowed the national government to call out the militia only "to execute the laws of the Union, suppress insurrections, or repel invasions." In no other circumstances could the general government assume power over the state militia. The council, therefore, advised that the governor "ought of right to retain the exclusive command of militia of this state." Finding neither the circumstances outlined in the Constitution nor a presidential proclamation declaring the threat of imminent invasion, the governor notified the War Department that "no portion of the militia of this state can, under existing circumstances, be withdrawn from [my] authority."[38]

Even had a presidential declaration been issued, Connecticut authorities questioned the constitutional basis for placing state militia units under the command of Regular Army officers. The

Constitution explicitly reserved to the states the power to appoint militia officers. Hence, Connecticut had appointed brigade, regimental, and battalion officers for the militia division readied in response to the federal quota assigned in April 1812. Dearborn's call for a battalion-size force, however, included the mobilization of only company-grade officers. In other words, the battalion officers appointed under state authority were left with commands in name only. To accept mobilization orders that dismissed part of the state-appointed officer corps, Connecticut argued, would concede to federal authorities the right to strip company-grade officers of their commands as well. If that could be done, any militia private could be separated from his militia company officers and transferred into the Army of the United States, leaving the state militia prerogatives meaningless. Dearborn's mobilization orders were unconstitutional, then, because they created a situation "impairing, if not annihilating, the militia itself, so sacredly guaranteed by the constitution to the several States."[39]

Massachusetts also questioned the constitutionality of the War Department's intention to place militia units under the command of Regular Army officers. Governor Caleb Strong and his council, guided by the justices of the state's supreme court, took the extreme position that only the President himself could command militia forces. The Constitution made the President Commander in Chief of the Army of the United States and the militia "when called into the actual service of the United States." Custom and law allowed the presidential command of the Regular Army to be exercised through a duly commissioned professional officer corps. In like manner, the President's command of the militia could be exercised only through its officer corps. "We know of no constitutional provision," noted the state supreme court, "authorizing any officer of the army of the United States to command the militia." To hold otherwise, "would render nugatory the provision that the militia are to have officers appointed by the states."[40]

More threatening, though, to the federal government's ability to provide for the common defense was Massachusett's position that the decision to place militia units in federal service belonged to the states. This view had been suggested by Rhode Island in the governor's brief letter to the Secretary of War. Both Rhode Island and Massachusetts went well beyond Connecticut's position that the militia could not be mobilized unless the federal government declared the need to execute the laws of the Union, suppress insurrection, or repel invasion.

The Constitution, Massachusetts argued, identified three purposes for which the state militias could be employed by the federal government, "but, no power is given, either to the President or to Congress, to determine, that either of the said exigencies do in fact exist."[41] And if the power was not delegated to the national government or prohibited to the states, it was reserved to the states to exercise through their governors, the commanders in chief of the militia.

State governors, then, had the power and responsibility to determine when their militias were obliged to enter federal service. Any other constitutional interpretation "would place all the militia, in effect, at the will of Congress." The governors' prerogatives were doubly important since Congress in 1795 had delegated to the President the authority to call out the militia to meet domestic and military emergencies. A President, if allowed to determine when such emergencies existed, could without congressional or state approval mobilize the militia to serve personal political or military ends. Such a consolidation of the militia system, state officials contended, was contrary "to the intentions of the people when, ratifying the Constitution."[42]

The reaction to Dearborn's mobilization orders surprised no one in the Madison administration. Nor should it have. Concern about the relative powers of the states and the general government in militia matters dated to the beginnings of the federal government. Despite repeated urgings from the executive branch, members of Congress had proved reluctant to establish a nationally integrated militia system. The debates leading up to the passage of the Militia Act of 1792 provided sound testimony to the determination of many to avoid what Massachusetts would call in 1812 "a military consolidation of the states."[43] The debate over the 1795 "Act to provide for calling forth the Militia to execute the Laws of the Union, to suppress insurrections, and repel invasion," which had its roots in legislation under the same title passed three years earlier, revealed deep concern about whether militia mobilization should be left to presidential discretion. Not surprisingly, even before the New England states rejected Dearborn's call for assistance, the Madison administration had considered its constitutional authority to call out the militia.

In June 1812, Secretary of the Treasury Albert Gallatin wrote

President James Madison delineating state and federal prerogatives in militia matters. The Constitution limited state authority
over the militia to training and appointing its officers, the former
Pennsylvania congressman argued. All other militia powers belonged to the general government. In particular, the President,
through the authority delegated by Congress in 1795, was empowered to call out the militia if the nation was threatened by
invasion, insurrection, or civil disobedience. State executives had
no constitutional authority to countermand such orders, argued
Gallatin. Moreover, governors, in their capacity as commander in
chief of their state's militia, had no independent authority over
state militia units once they were called into the field. State
executives assuming personal command of state forces, like other
militia officers, had "to obey the orders of the President; he is
their Commander in Chief."[44]

It was not until the war ended, however, that the Madison
administration addressed fully the issues raised by the New England states. During the war years, the War Department largely
ignored the pronouncements of the New England governors,
raising what New England troops it could through the Volunteer
Act of February 1812. Nevertheless, when in early 1815 a Senate
committee sought advice concerning a possible legislative solution
to federal-state differences over militia mobilization, the administration used the opportunity to respond to the constitutional
issues raised by Massachusetts and Connecticut two and one-half
years before: Could the President call out the militia without state
executive approval? and could the militia be organized under the
command of Regular Army officers? "These being," Secretary of
State James Monroe noted, "the only difficulties which have
arisen between the Executives of the United States and the executives of any of the individual states, relative to the command of
the militia."[45]

While conceding the importace of the rights reserved to the
states, Monroe considered the position taken by New England
states to be "repugnant" to the principles upon which the Constitution was based. "The power . . . given to Congress . . . to provide for calling forth the militia for the purposes specified in the
constitution, is unconditional." "It was obvious," Monroe told the
Senate committee, that the Framers of the Constitution intended
that the militia power "vested in the General Government, should
be independent of the states' authorities." Federal law could not

be enforced if state executives could withhold the militia from national service; neither could insurrections be put down. Finally, if denied access to the militia when faced by a threatened or actual invasion, the national government would have no recourse but to maintain a large and expensive Regular Army. Indeed, the United States would be forced "to resort to standing armies for all national purposes." That, thought Monroe, was a policy so "fraught with mischief, and so absurd" that it could not be "imputed to a free people in this enlighted age." It could not have been the intention of the Framers of the Constitution or "the good people of these states" when they ratified the document.

Monroe pointed to past practice and legislative authority to support the executive branch's interpretation of the Constitution. The Washington administration's early and ongoing interest in the creation of national militia structure underscored that the government was built on the assumption that the militia was "principally to be relied on for all national purposes." Monroe also noted that Washington "relied exclusively on the powers of the General Government" to put down the Whiskey Rebellion in 1794. The President did not ask authorities in Pennsylvania to certify that an insurrection was under way before mobilizing militia units in that and neighboring states. Neither were affected state executives consulted before their troops were called into federal service. Still, the states cooperated. Partisanship, Monroe implied, more than constitutional differences had shaped New England's wartime militia policy. No state official had challenged either the 1792 or 1795 legislation authorizing the President to call out the militia "without any communication with, or reference to, the executives of the individual states" until the "late unhappy differences . . . New England states."

Massachusetts' claim that only the President could command militia units in federal service Monroe found incomprehensible. "That the President alone had a right to command the militia . . . and that no officer of the Regular Army can take the command in his absence, is a construction for which I can see nothing in the constitution to afford the slightest pretext." As Commander in Chief of the militia and of the land and naval forces of the United States, the President controlled the operations of American forces. Nevertheless, he was not required to take the field in person. The notion advanced by the Bay State's justices that a unified militia command depended on the presence of the President pushed "the doctrine of state rights" to the point of absurdity. Independent allies threatened by a common enemy might choose to unite their armies under a commonly agreed-upon commander, but the situation in the United States was different. "The President is himself no bond of union," Monroe pointed out. He is but the Commander in Chief "under a constitution which binds us together as one people."

New England's interpretation of the Constitution threatened to undermine the general government's ability to provide for the common defense, Monroe told the Senate committee, radically altering both the character and responsibilities of the national government. In his view, all state authority ceased once the militia was called out for federal service. That the states appointed officers and trained the militia had "no effect on the character and duties of the militia, when called into the service of the United States." Militia officers and soldiers, like their Regular Army counterparts, were part of a national force, paid and commanded by the general government. "There is but one power and one government, and the troops, whether regular or militia, though distinguished by shades of character, constitute but one people, and are, in fact, countrymen, friends, and bretheren." If the President or the War Department chose to integrate the militia into a Regular Army command, neither state officials nor militia soldiers were in a position to object.

The Senate committee accepted Monroe's argument, declining to propose legislation addressing New England's concerns. Nevertheless, another decade passed before the constitutional questions raised during the war years were settled. Massachusetts formally abandoned its wartime stand early in 1824 after extended negotiations with Congress and the executive branch over the payment of claims based on state-directed militia service during the War of 1812. Pointing to "an unhallowed spirit of party" and speaking of the "unwarrantable course pursued by this state, during the late war," Massachusetts' governor, senate, and house of representatives conceded that the policies arising from its interpretation of the Constitution had "subjected [the national] government to the uncertain and irresponsible opinions, of the commanders in chief of the several states." Worse, it had "effectively deprived the National Government of all means of enforcing the laws of the nation, without the previous consent of the [state] commanders in chief, unless by a standing army."[46]

The United States Supreme Court lent its authority to the executive branch's interpretation of its militia power three years later. In *Martin v. Mott*, a case that grew out of a New York militiaman's refusal to enter federal service, the Marshall Court ruled unanimously that the authority to call out the militia for the purposes outlined in the Constitution "belongs exclusively to the President, and that his decision is conclusive upon all other persons."[47]

Writing for the Court, Justice Joseph Story affirmed the constitutionality of the 1795 legislation delegating authority over militia mobilization to the President. He also considered beyond debate the act's provision for the President to exercise that authority when faced with the threat of invasion as well as actual attack. "In our opinion," wrote Story, "the power to provide for repelling invasions includes the power to provide against the attempt and danger of invasion, as the necessary and proper means to effectuate the object." The Court was equally certain that the President alone held the power to determine when circumstances warranted federal militia service. Any other interpretation, Story contended, would allow every militia officer and soldier—from state commander in chief to county conscript—to "refuse to obey the orders of the President."

The Court's opinion turned on the nature and purpose of the power exercised by the President. The Framers of the Constitution, wrote Justice Story, expected the national government to use the militia during "sudden emergencies, upon great occasions of state, and under circumstances which may be vital to the existence of the Union." Indeed, not until 1807 did federal statutes allow the use of Regular Army or Naval personnel to enforce laws or maintain public order. While conceding that the power to mobilize the militia was "one of no ordinary magnitude," the Court held that a prompt and unhesitating obedience to orders is indispensable" to the fulfillment of any military prerogative. Delays threatened the public interest. "While subordinate officers and soldiers are pausing to consider whether they ought to obey, or are scrupulously weighing the evidence of the facts upon which the commander-in-chief exercises the right to demand their services, the hostile enterprise may be accomplished without means of resistance."

The Supreme Court, citing a recent New York court decision, affirmed that when exercising legitimate authority, "every public officer is presumed to act in obedience to his duty." This ruling was particularly important in military matters, Story argued. The national government could not carry out its responsibility to provide for the common defense if the legitimacy of presidential orders was subject to the scrutiny of a jury. Worse, exposing every officer who obeyed presidential commands to "ruinous litigation" would destroy discipline in the ranks and drive the "best disposed officers" from federal service.

From the Court's perspective, the 1795 militia mobilization act merely implemented the powers outlined in Article I, Section 8, of the Constitution. By giving the President the exclusive authority to call out the militia, Congress recognized that the threat of an invasion was not always reducible to evidence that would constitute a "strict technical proof" in a court of law. Moreover, disclosure of the evidence for an invasion "might reveal important secrets of state, which the public interest, and even safety, might imperiously demand to be kept in concealment." Concerns that the President might abuse the authority delegated to him bore not at all on the constitutionality of his prerogatives, Story argued. Any power could be abused; besides the Constitution provided for impeachment in the event of official misconduct. The republican form of government, declared the Court, assumed that the President possessed "public virtue and [an] honest devotion to the public interests" and that frequent elections and the watchful eye of Congress would "guard against usurpations or wanton tyranny."

The Supreme Court's decision in *Martin* v. *Mott* closed the debate over the control of the militia under the federal system established by the Constitution. At the heart of the Court's decision was the belief that an effective military system required centralization and executive leadership. Moreover, the Court insisted that the exercise of military powers in a republican government depended on an element of trust. The federal government benefited little, however, from the confirmation of its authority to call out the states' militias. Like England more than a century earlier, the final round fought between national and local authorities over militia prerogatives was done at a time when that organization of citizen-soldiers had largely ceased to function. Only months before the Supreme Court handed down its decision in *Martin* v. *Mott*, a board of Regular and militia officers reported to the Secretary of War that though "An amendment to the Constitution . . . consecrates the great principle 'that a well-regulated militia being necessary to the security of a free state, the right of the people to keep and bear arms shall not be infringed,'" the militia was neither well regulated nor ably armed.[48] The Marshall Court had, as it did in other decisions, confirmed for the national government an important power, but one the full implications of which for the Republic's constitutional order awaited the twentieth century. Not until Congress created the National Guard in the aftermath of the Spanish-American War would the full implications of *Martin* v. *Mott* be known.

Notes

1. Edward I, c. 3 (1279), in Great Britain, *Statutes at Large [1225–1676]* compiled by Joseph Keble (London, 1676), 33.

2. Edward III, c. 3 (1328), ibid., 91.

3. Richard II, c. 13 (1383) and 20 Richard II, c. 1 (1396), in ibid., 167, 187.

4. William Hawkins, *A Treatise of the Pleas of the Crown* (London, 1724–26), 135–36.

5. 11 Henry VIII, c. 15 (1494) and 19 Henry VIII, c. 1 (1503), Keble, comp., *Statutes at Large*, 323, 331.

6. Lindsay Boynton, *The Elizabethan Militia, 1588–1638* (London, 1967), passim. Lois G. Schwoerer, *"No Standing Armies!" The Antiarmy Ideology of Seventeenth-Century-England* (Baltimore, 1974), 12–15.

7. See Lois G. Schwoerer, "The Fittest Subject for A King's Quarrel: An Essay on the Military Controversy 1641–1642," *Journal of British Studies* 11 (1971): 46–76, for a complete discussion of the constitutional issues raised in 1641 and 1642.

8. Anonymous, *An Answer or Necessary Animadversions, upon Some late Impostumate Observations invective against his Sacred Majesty* (London, 1642), 20.

9. Parker, *Observations upon some of his Majesties late Answers and Expresses* (London, 1642), 1–4, 13–15.

10. Quoted in Schwoerer, "The Fittest Subject for a King's Quarrel," *Journal of British Studies* 11 (1971):70–71.

11. John March, *An Argument or Debate in Law: of the Great Question concerning the Militia* (London, 1642), 1–42.

12. Anonymous, *Peaceable Militia or the Cause and Cure of the Late and Present Warre* (London, 1648), 10–12, 15–17. This is the first essay to advocate the locally controlled militia as the surest protection against the misuses of centralized military power.

13. Schwoerer, *"No Standing Armies!"* 62–64.

14. Schwoerer, *"No Standing Armies!"* 82–90. John B. Western, *The English Militia in the Eighteenth Century: The Story of a Political Issue, 1660–1802* (London, 1965), 7–8.

15. Schwoerer, *"No Standing Armies!"* 62–66. John Childs, *The Army of Charles II* (London, 1976), 218–19.

16. John Miller, *The Army, James II, and the Glorius Revolution* (New York, 1980), 6–10, 19–23. Miller, "The Militia and the Army in the Reign of James II," *The Historical Journal* 16 (1973): 659–69.

17. Bernard Schwartz, ed., *The Roots of the Bill of Rights* (New York, 1980), 1: 42–43. 22 Charles II, c. 25 (1670), in Keble, comp., *Statutes at Large*, 1009. See Robert Shalhope, "The Ideological Origins of the Second Amendment," *Journal of American History* 69 (1982): 602–604, for a different view.

18. This discussion of the state and national constitutions appeared in expanded form in Lawrence D. Cress, *Citizens in Arms: The Army and Militia in American Society to the War of 1812* (Chapel Hill, 1982), 60–66 and 94–109.

19. The relevant constitutional provisions are Article 1, Sections 8 and 9, and Article 2, Section 2.

20. Luther Martin, *Genuine Information . . .*, delivered to the Maryland legislature, 29 November 1787, Max Farrand, ed., *Records of the Federal Convention of 1787* (New Haven, 1937) 3: 268–69.

21. Patrick Henry, Virginia Convention, 5 June 1788, Jonathan Elliot, ed., *Debates in the Several State Conventions on the Adoption of the Federal Constitution* (Philadelphia, 1896) 3: 47–48, 51–52.

22. *Annals of Congress*, 1st Cong., 1st sess., pp. 778–80.

23. [Hamilton], *Federalist 6, 8, 16, 21, 25, 75*, in Jacob E. Cooke, ed., *The Federalist* (Middletown Ct., 1961), 28–36, 44–47, 99–102, 103–32, 158–60, 588.

24. "The Republican," *Connecticut Courant*, 7 January 1788.

25. [Hamilton], *Federalist No. 29*, in Cooke, ed., *The Federalist*, 181–85.

26. Madison, Virginia Convention, 16 June 1788, *Debates in the Several State Conventions*, 3: 413.

27. Thomas Dawes, Massachusetts Convention, 24 January 1788, ibid., 2: 98.

28. Webster, *An Examination . . .*, Paul Leicester Ford, ed., *Pamphlets on the Constitution of the United States . . ., 1787–1788* (Brooklyn, 1888), 56–57.

29. [Madison], *Federalist No. 46*, in Cooke, ed., *The Federalist*, 321–22.

30. See Lawrence D. Cress, "An Armed Community: The Origins and Meaning of the Right to Bear Arms," *Journal of American History* 71 (1984): 22–42, for a full discussion of the development of the Second Amendment.

31. *Debates in the Several State Conventions*, 1: 335.

32. Ibid., 3: 659–60.

33. *Annals of Congress*, 1st Cong., 1st sess., 451, 685–91, 778. Schwartz, ed., *Roots of the Bill of Rights*, 5, illustration following p. 1014.

34. *Annals of Congress*, 1st Cong., 1st sess., pp. 778–81.

35. Schwartz, ed., *Roots of the Bill of Rights*, 5: 1149, 1122, 1153–54.

36. J. C. A. Stagg, *Mr. Madison's War: Politics, Diplomacy, and Warfare in the Early Republic, 1783–1830* (Princeton, 1983), 258–59. Reginald Horsman, *The War of 1812* (New York, 1969), 3031. John K. Mahon, *The War of 1812* (Gainesville, 1972), 32–33.

37. William Jones to William Eustis, 18 June 1812 and 22 August 1812, Walter Louise and Matthew S. Clarke, eds., *American State Papers, Military Affairs* (Washington, 1838) 1: 621.

38. John Cotton Smith to William Eustis, 2 July 1812, ibid., 615. The Resolutions of the Connecticut Council, n.d., quoted in *Norfolk Gazette*, 8 July 1812. Resolutions of the Connecticut Council, 4 August 1812, in ibid., 17 August 1812. Proclamation of Governor Roger Griswold, 6 August 1812, in ibid., quoting the Declaration of the Connecticut Council.

39. Ibid.

40. Caleb Strong to William Eustis, 5 August 1812; Theophilus Parsons, Samuel Sewall, and Isaac Parker [Justices of the Supreme Judicial Court], to Caleb Strong, n.d., *House Documents*, 18th Cong., 1st sess., no. 83, 137–39, 140–42.

41. Parsons, Sewall, and Parker to Strong, n.d., *House Documents*, 18th Cong., 1st sess., no. 83, 140–41.

42. Ibid.

43. Parsons, Sewall, and Parker to Strong, n.d., *House Documents*, 18th Cong., 1st sess., no. 83, 140–41.

44. [Gallatin] to Madison, June 1812, Gallatin Papers, roll 25, New York University.

45. Monroe's analysis is in a letter to William G. Giles, 11 February 1815. *House Documents*, 18th Cong., 1st sess., no. 83, 127–33.

46. George Sullivan to John C. Calhoun, 23 February 1824; Speech of Governor Eustis to the Legislature of Massachusetts [May Session, 1823]; Answer of the

House of Representatives, of Massachusetts, to the Governor's Speech; Answer of the Senate of Massachusetts to Governor Eustis's Speech, May Session 1823. *House Documents*, 18th Cong., 1st sess., no. 83, 105–116.
47. *Martin v. Mott*, 6 *Law. Ed.* 537–44 (1827).
48. Report of the Board of Officers Relative to the Militia to James Barbour, November 28, 1826, *American State Papers, Military Affairs*, 3: 388–92.

The Constitution and the Citizen: The Question of Civilian Control

by

William A. Stofft

Critics often comment on the constitutional illiteracy of the American public; and isn't it true that only a few can recall even the opening phrases of the Constitution's Preamble or perhaps the words of its First Amendment? But in countless ways Americans demonstrate a lively understanding of the meaning of constitutionalism. Examples abound of our assumption that the Constitution represents a contract between the citizen and the government. We speak ceaselessly, it would seem, of rights and privileges, and somehow we sense in our bones that these rights and privileges have constitutional origins.

One of these commonly held assumptions—that the Constitution guarantees subordination of the nation's military forces to civil authority—has been questioned by a famous American scholar. In 1976 Samuel P. Huntington posited that "despite the widespread popular belief to the contrary, the Constitution does *not* provide for civilian control."[1]

Huntington is a political scientist, and his primary interest centered on civil-military relations and military security in the late twentieth century, but in developing his thesis, he had much to say about the relation between the professional soldier and the citizen at the birth of the Republic.

In drawing up the military sections of the Constitution, Huntington concluded, the Framers, as elsewhere, were strongly influenced by their view of the British Civil War and the Glorious Revolution of the previous century. Their primary concern was the possibility of governmental powers being illegally assumed by some citizen or group of citizens. In other words, their aim was not to guard against unchecked military force, but to create a balance of power among those who would govern. The Constitution they devised did not address the question of the place of the military in American society, but established a system of checks and balances that diluted the power of any individual or group by dividing governmental responsibility and control, including control over the military.

But while the Framers feared the misuse of military power by national and state governments, Huntington argued, they betrayed no special concern for the usurpation of power by a professional soldier class. This too, he pointed out, reflected the Framers' view of history. Life in the American colonies had not lent itself to the rise of a professional military class. The concept of the citizen-soldier, grafted from English roots, not only encompassed the American ideal, but characterized all military service up to the time of the Revolution. Huntington would consider Cincinnatus an appropriate symbol for the American soldier, a symbol personified by George Washington, the planter-citizen turned soldier-statesman. In the Constitution, Huntington concluded, the Framers perpetuated the colonial idea of the citizen-soldier as the usual, but not necessarily exclusive, expression of military power. The question of military subordination was, therefore, extraneous to the debate in the Convention, and, as a civil liberty, must trace its origin to extraconstitutional sources.

Huntington is of course correct when he points out that the Constitution does not explicitly define the subordinate relationship of the military to the civilian powers, but I think a reasonable case can be made for the claim that the idea does have a constitutional origin. A survey of the period, it seems to me, demonstrates that if the Framers had as yet no personal experience of a native professional military class, they nevertheless betrayed a keen awareness of the potential danger of such a caste; that their concern about such a power group was included in their worry about all power groups during the debates in Philadelphia; that their determination to guarantee civilian supremacy pervades what they wrote in the military clauses of the Constitution; and that their intent to use the Constitution to protect the nation against such dangers was further spelled out during the early years of the new Republic in the nation's first military laws.

A heightened anxiety over the danger of a professional military class trampling the rights of citizens permeates the Revolutionary generation. It was ushered in by the presence of British troops in North America operating independently of colonial legislatures in the decade of tension prior to 1776. Americans could see no valid military reason for the stationing of British regiments in their midst and assumed that the only reason for their presence was to enforce unpopular parliamentary measures, in particular the Intolerable Acts. However overblown the rhetoric that surrounded the Boston Massacre may have been, that disturbance nevertheless impressed on the colonies the idea of citizens dying at the hands of unconstitutional troops, who themselves were obeying a military governor (the Commander in Chief of North America).

During those troubled times, Americans still generally clung to the idea that they were Englishmen who lived overseas, but the specter of redcoated officers in Boston and elsewhere arrogantly ignoring what the colonists increasingly referred to as the "traditional rights of the British citizen," was rapidly eroding that belief. The exercise of military power uncontrolled by the representatives of the people served as a proximate cause of the Revolution, but also accounted for the passage of some of the newly independent nation's earliest military laws, laws supported by almost every shade of political opinion.[2]

These concerns were exacerbated during the Revolution and in the years before the Framers met in Philadelphia. Three specific events in particular occurred during this time to heighten the public's anxiety quotient over the possibility of military ascendancy.

George Washington unwittingly introduced the issue himself during the dark winter of 1777 in Valley Forge. Beset by problems associated with transforming a ragtag army into a force capable of meeting the world's best professionals on the battlefield, he also faced the very real possibility of losing his experienced officers, many of whom could no longer afford the financial losses connected with continued military service. Meeting with a congressional delegation led by Francis Dana and Gouverneur Morris, Washington proposed that Congress borrow a leaf from the British and offer Continental officers, as an inducement to serve for the duration, a lifetime pension amounting to half their active pay.[3]

His proposal set off a firestorm in the states and in Congress, where opponents charged that such an expenditure would create—in the words of one anxious delegate—"a set of haughty idle imperious Scandalizers of industrious Citizens and Farmers."[4] Rejected in April 1778 as originally proposed, a considerably modified version was eventually accepted by Congress after extensive lobbying by the Commander in Chief. In the end, Congress agreed to grant officers serving for the duration seven years of half pay, but added a lump sum payment of eighty dollars for those enlistedmen who also stayed the course.

The compromise did not still congressional fears. During the many weeks of debate, delegates thoroughly aired the widespread public fear of a professional officer class and the danger it posed to the citizenry. Many delegates considered the request for half pay, in the words of Henry Laurens, the president of the Congress, "unjust & unconstitutional in its nature & full of dangerous consequences."[5] In summing up the objections of those who feared the passage of the measure, Laurens wrote that the people were being reduced to the awful alternative of either losing their army or their liberties. The pension idea would be dangerous, he concluded, "because it would be establishing a precedent to the Soldiery . . . because the people would have no security against future arbitrary demands—because the attempt is to deprive the Representative of free Agency & to reduce that Body to a State of subserviency—because it would lay the foundations of a standing Army, of an Aristocracy, the demand militates against the Articles of Confederation."[6] Even in the darkest days of a war for national survival, it would seem, concern with nuances of civil-military relations and fears for what a professional military class might portend proved of paramount interest to the representatives of the people.

A second issue concerning the question of civilian supremacy centered around what historian Don Higginbotham has called "the uproar over the Society of the Cincinnati."[7] That society, founded in the closing months of the war by Henry Knox, Frederick Steuben, and others, was a fraternal organization opened to officers of the Continental Army who had served for three years or who were on active duty at the cessation of hostilities. General Washington himself had accepted appointment as first president-general of the society, but even the association of the nation's premier hero could not save the group from widespread criticism and the country from another debate over civil-military relations.

The criticism, which ranged across the political spectrum,

centered on the society's bylaws. One of these laws limited future membership in the group to the oldest male descendent of each veteran. This, many feared, would lead to the formation of a new American aristocracy akin to France's "nobility of the sword." Such a special class of citizen, set apart somehow by heredity, seemed at wide variance with the ideas of the new American society that was self-consciously espousing the simple virtues of republicanism.

But if hereditary membership caused a philosophical dispute, other bylaws were even more worrying to a nation sensitive to civilian control. The society's rules divided the group into thirteen separate state organizations and a special chapter in France. These separate units were to communicate by means of a newsletter in which not only society business, but information about "the general union of the states" would be circulated. These plans—along with news that the society was forming a general fund to support its undefined charitable interests—appeared altogether sinister to critics, raising the fear that well-financed veterans, operating from cells in every state, would be strategically placed to launch a scheme to alter the republican form of government. A committee of the Massachusetts legislature called the society "unjustifiable, and if not properly discountenanced may be dangerous to the peace, liberty, and safety of the United States in General, and this Commonwealth in particular."[8] Although interest in the society's affairs subsided after the group promised to change its rules, allusions to the society and military control of the government could be seen in the press and in political discourse up to the eve of the Constitutional Convention.

Too much can be made of this commotion, but in New England especially, concern over the machinations of veterans organized in such a national group that had somehow become coupled in the public's mind with veterans' demands for pensions did much to fuel Antinationalist sentiments in the immediate postwar period. It also provided staunch republicans like Elbridge Gerry a vehicle to ride back into national politics. Gerry in particular was able to blend the people's suspicions of a hereditary veterans' society with his own particular concern over standing armies to the detriment of plans for a small national army in the postwar years.[9]

Discontent in the Continental Army over bread and butter issues led to the third, and most serious, civil-military crisis in the

decade. As the war wound down to its final months, a few officers
on duty in the main army headquartered at Newburgh, New
York, prepared a series of petitions, or addresses, purporting to
represent the demands of the entire Continental Army officer
corps, concerning unpaid salaries and the promise of pensions.
Willing to compromise the victory won in the earlier half-pay
issue, these officers were ready to settle for payment of back
salary and some lump sun grant in lieu of a pension.[10]

Washington himself fully sympathized with the financial
plight of his men and declared their quest for remuneration just.
But for all the seeming reasonableness of their claims, their petitions to Congress were little more than a veiled threat. They were
determined, they reported, not to disband the Army until they
had "obtained justice," that is, until these money matters were
settled to their satisfaction. As Maj. John Armstrong, Jr., an aide
to Maj. Gen. Horatio Gates and author of the first petition, hinted
darkly: "any further experiments on their [the soldiers'] patience
may have fatal effects."

Remarks freely circulated to the effect that the Army was
attempting to bolster the hand of Congress, winning from the
states further power to impose taxes and thereby secure for the
Army the financial assistance it demanded. Here, the calculating
figure of Alexander Hamilton could be detected behind the
scenes. Although he was apparently more interested in using the
occasion to advance the interests of the Nationalists in Congress,
Hamilton's sympathetic reception of the petition was enough to
chill the hearts of the Antinationalists.

Washington himself certainly considered the threat serious.
Fearing an outright rebellion, he acted swiftly yet cautiously. In
the first place his control over the situation depended on his
retaining the respect and loyalty of his officers and men. But
such moral suasion depended in part on his willingness to fight
for their just causes. At the same time, he was determined to
uphold the supremacy of the civilian government.

He decided on a direct confrontation that would enable him to
capitalize on his subordinates' loyalty. Meeting on March 15,
1783, with officers from every unit stationed near Newburgh,
Washington began by strongly attacking their petition, raising
the specter of treason to men who had just fought a successful war
against untrammeled military tyranny. He asked them bluntly if
the Army could ever consider turning on Congress, thereby "plot-

ting the ruin of both, by sowing the seeds of discord and separation" between the soldier and his civilian superiors. Then in a moment of high theatre that devastated his audience, the venerable general fumbled for his new eyeglasses to read them a letter, remarking "Gentlemen, you will permit me to put on my spectacles, for I have not only grown gray but almost blind in the service of my country." This dramatic performance, which artfully combined his charge of treason with an outright appeal to the Army's love for its commander, completely disarmed the potential rebellion. In reply, the officers reaffirmed their confidence in Congress and in effect rejected their own petitions.

Some historians have since belittled the standard interpretation of the Newburgh conspiracy, calling it but a minor episode in the Nationalists' scheme to strengthen the central government by enhancing its taxation powers and, at any event, little more than a simple petition of grievances. Any threat to civilian government, they claim, if it existed at all, was largely rhetorical, since it was so easily neutralized by Washington.

But this assertion flies in the face of Washington's obvious concern. More important for this discussion, the officers' addresses and Washington's response were common knowledge throughout the country in a matter of weeks. In Congress the reaction was similar to that following the half-pay and Cincinnati controversies. Delegate James Madison called it "alarming intelligence" and reported that the news had caused "peculiar awe and solemnity . . . and oppressed the minds of Cong[res]s with an anxiety and distress which had been scarcely felt in any period of the revolution."[11]

The political concern aroused by these three events may have had little lasting effect on the military plans of the Nationalists, but it did add to the larger national legacy of concern over military power that traces back to the Redcoats in the years before the Revolution. And these events had constitutional consequences. My colleague Richard Kohn points out that the implications of a conflict between Congress and the Army worried leaders in both institutions during the war. He explains that although both sides "had striven mightily to preserve the form and the substance of military subordination," there existed few precedents on the national level for such a tradition. The British system, where an aristocratic class traditionally manned leadership positions in both the government and the Army, would never work in America with its strong citizen-soldier tradition. So the idea of a professional military class subordinate to civilian government was new in America and, he concludes, extremely vulnerable.[12] Reaction to these three events demonstrated a general awareness of this constitutional issue. It also can safely be assumed that concern over civil-military relations was part of the intellectual baggage brought by the delegates to Philadelphia in 1787.

It has been asserted with considerable justification that the meeting in Philadelphia in the hot summer of 1787 was in the main a quest for government balance: a balance between state and national government; between branches of the national government; and a balance of governmental functions and powers. This balance seemed capable of infinite subdivision. Even the military clauses written by the Framers reflect an overriding concern with a balance of forces and a balance of controls. A majority of the delegates had been involved in the prosecution of the War for Independence, on the battlefield, in Congress, or in state governments. That formative influence provided a crucial frame of reference during their discussion of military affairs. Delegates were not dealing in theory but reflecting personal experiences. But while they assumed that the need for security in its broadest context provides the fundamental reason for any government's existence, they also feared military dictatorship.

Although the subject of military subordination was rarely mentioned during Convention debate over military matters, it can be reasonably deduced that, so total was the agreement among the Framers on the subject, they felt no need to address the question in any specific way. This total agreement was ineluctably linked to the delegates' perception of the character of their presiding officer. It was a foregone conclusion that George Washington would assume the office of chief executive in any new republic fashioned by the Convention, and many of the fears that the Framers may have entertained about the role of the military in a democratic society were stilled by their perception of the nation's premier citizen and soldier. Both in deed and word, Washington had demonstrated again and again his keen awareness of the problems associated with the exercise of military power in a democratic society.

This was not always the case. Don Higginbotham points out that as a young militia colonel in Braddock's campaign, Washington could fulminate with the best of them over the shortcomings of the civilian government. But, Higginbotham goes on to explain, the seventeen years that separate the fiery young colonel from the mature general who took charge of American forces around Boston in 1775 were years of important tuition. Washington's legislative experience during those years wrought a great transformation in his attitude toward representative government. In Higginbotham's words: "His respect for and understanding of superior authority—that is to say, civil control of the military *and all that it meant*—became his most admirable soldierly quality in the War of Independence and his foremost contribution to the American military tradition."[13]

Washington was selected Commander in Chief, not for his military abilities, for several others had more experience in the profession of arms—but because his fellow legislators knew and trusted him as a legislator representing a key Southern state. Never, throughout the war, did he abuse this trust in any way. Richard Kohn has summarized the judgment of the historical community: "But most of all, Washington should be remembered and appreciated for his absolute, unconditional, and steadfast refusal ever to seek or seize power outside legitimate political or constitutional channels."[14] Despite the myriad trials with a Congress jealous of its prerogatives but unsure of its obligations, Washington remained scrupulous in his relations with the civil authority and never took advantage of his position as national hero to thwart the will of the delegates. As Kohn put it: "From the very beginning of his command, respect for civil authority was his first principle."

Washington's greatest contribution to the Revolution was his character as a man. In the day-to-day conduct of the war, he faced almost insurmountable difficulties in dealing with an often ineffectual Congress. Yet never, in any instance, did he betray the trust that Congress had placed in him. He always kept the members informed of his plans and made it evident to even the most suspicious of critics that, as long as he remained in command, the Continental Army was no threat to Congress' authority nor to the liberties of the citizenry. He made his intentions clear in his oft-quoted remarks to the New York Assembly in 1775: "When we assumed the Soldier, we did not lay aside the Citizen; and we shall most sincerely rejoice with you in that happy hour when the establishment of American Liberty, upon the most firm and solid foundations, shall enable us to return to our Private Stations in the bosom of a free, peaceful and happy Country." To a large extent, the key to the Revolution's success was trust. Trust was needed to forge a new nation out of thirteen separate and often mutually jealous states and preserve the consent of a citizenry that represented every shade of political and economic opinion. The success of the enterprise depended in great part on the growing trust these groups developed under the leadership of their citizen-general.

Washington's actions during the war demonstrated that a professional military force was not necessarily a danger to the citizens' liberties. His writings on the subject after the war sought to demonstrate to his fellow citizens that a standing army in time of peace was both necessary and compatible with popular republican views. In November 1783 he issued his farewell orders to the Continental Army. Urging his men, most with strong attachments to the Union, to carry back into civilian society "the most conciliating dispositions," he reminded them that their private virtues as civilians must match the qualities of valor, perseverance, and enterprise they had showed in uniform. He repeated his "frequently given" opinion to his soldiers that "unless the principles of the federal government were properly supported and the powers of the Union increased, the honor, dignity, and justice of the nation would be lost forever."[15] Above all, Washington recognized that the American soldier was first and foremost a citizen, with all the duties and rights enjoyed by others, not someone outside the mainstream of society.

One final quote from this most quotable of men refers directly to the lingering fears over military power. When asked to provide his sentiments on a peace establishment, Washington said: "Altho' a *large* standing Army in time of Peace hath ever been considered dangerous to the liberties of a Country, yet a few Troops, under certain circumstances are not only safe, but indispensably necessary."[16] It is only a slight exaggeration to assert that the Framers sought to enshrine the philosophy and character of this epitome of the citizen-soldier and soldier-statesman into the military clauses of the Constitution.

Washington's presence at the Convention and the sure knowledge that he would be selected to guide the new government defused much of the concern over civil-military relations. Nevertheless, it is also readily apparent that commonly held assumptions about the necessity of civilian control were used to support arguments in the larger debate over standing armies. That shibboleth—for shibboleth it had surely become in a Confederation that had already given its blessing to the raising of a small force of regulars—remained in the spotlight throughout the Convention and during the ratification period that followed. In fact, the question of civilian control remained the philosophical basis in all the debate over standing armies, and the phrase "standing armies" could well be understood as political shorthand for those long-rehearsed fears about losing control of military forces.

The Framers' solution to the problem of standing armies and their control, like their solution to other controversial issues elsewhere in the Constitution, was the creation of a system of checks and balances. A brief survey of the debate over the military clauses, it seems to me, clearly demonstrates that the quest for balance very much involved the question of civilian supremacy, and that the system devised in Philadelphia created a balance between security and control that has survived for two hundred years.

Both comprehensive plans of government introduced to the Convention on May 29, 1787 by the Virginia delegation and Charles Pinckney of South Carolina cited the need for explicit national authority over the means of defense.[17] Their scheme for military control went unchallenged until the line-by-line analysis of the work was debated in the Committee of Detail. There, three objections were aired. The first, involving the right of the national government to subdue rebellion, was actually part of the states rights argument over the introduction of federal troops in state affairs. A second, on the power to make war, addressed the distribution of powers between the legislative and executive branches. But the third involved the question of the threat of a standing army. Elbridge Gerry and Luther Martin, both ardent Antifederalists, sought to insert an explicit limit on the number of Regular troops that could be maintained in peacetime, employing once again the familiar arguments about the dangers of a standing army and military subordination. Judging by accounts left by several delegates, Washington glowered at Gerry, thereby sparking a rush to reject the amendment by delegates who had once served under the old commander.

What should not be overlooked in this exchange, is that even Gerry, the Cassandra of the Convention, did not object to the premise that the central government could establish a peacetime

military force. His acceptance pointed to the Convention's being
in the process of achieving an acceptable balance in military
forces and a system that guaranteed its control by the civilian
government.

In reaching an agreement over the constitutionality of a national military force, the Framers had considered two different
approaches. One, reflecting the experience of the Continental
Army and Washington's strong recommendations, held that the
nation needed a professionally trained, full-time army capable of
defeating an organized enemy on the battlefield; the other emphasized the traditional role of the citizen-soldier, the militiaman
locally trained to defend his home and region. Seeking as broad a
consensus as possible, the Convention chose to employ elements
of both.

But what about civilian control? The remedies devised by the
Framers to guarantee its preservation can be isolated in the Constitution. The issue was specifically raised on August 20 when
Charles Cotesworth Pinckney, the South Carolina Nationalist and
Continental Army veteran, recommended a series of propositions
to be included in the Constitution, including one that read: "The
military shall always be subordinate to the Civil power, and no
grants of money shall be made by the Legislature for supporting
military Land forces, for more than one year at a time." Pinckney
also recommended inclusion of a provision forbidding the President and others, including the Secretaries of Marine and War,
from "holding any other office of Trust or Emolument under the
U.S. or an individual State."[18] In effect, he sought to bar serving
military officers from top federal positions. These propositions
were referred to the Committee of Detail and some, in modified
form, found their way into the final draft.

Gouverneur Morris, another Nationalist and veteran of the
Revolution, also submitted a series of propositions, two of which
provided his solution to the question of civilian control. Morris
wanted the Constitution to stipulate that the Secretaries of War
and Marine would be appointed by the President and serve at his
pleasure. These officials, his went on, would superintend everything relating to their departments, such as raising and equipping forces, caring for military fortifications, arsenals, and the
like, and "in time of war to prepare and recommend plans of
offense and defense."[19] In effect, Morris wanted the Constitution
to place all these considerable powers explicitly in the hands of

civilian officials.

In the end the delegates agreed that these propositions guaranteeing the subordination of the military did not need explicit expression in the final document. Instead they resolved the thorny issue of potential abuses of military power by inserting the Army, Navy, and militia into the same carefully structured set of checks and balances that appear throughout the Constitution. To promote military efficiency, the Framers provided for the creation of a professional military force under the control of the national government. At the same time they balanced this new institution by providing for the continuation of the much larger militia that would, except in times of national emergency, remain under control of the individual states. Furthering this division of power, the Framers provided that the separate states retain the authority to appoint their militia officers and to supervise the peacetime training of their citizen-soldiers.

The delegates were able to create a standing army by establishing a much tighter civilian control over the armed forces than existed in almost any contemporary European country. Although, as Huntington correctly observed, they carefully divided this civilian control, the Framers nevertheless made clear that at every level the military was to be subordinate. The Constitution they devised made the civilian President Commander in Chief of the nation's military forces, including militiamen on federal duty, and then turned around and invested in Congress exclusively the key right to "provide for the common defense." Specifically, it gave the national legislature the power to declare war and to provide for calling forth the militia. In the vital area of finances, it gave the House of Representatives the power to initiate measures to raise and support armies, and, as further assurance that the legislature would remain a full partner of the executive in control of the military forces, it limited all military appropriations to two-year periods. The Constitution barred military officers from serving in Congress, and provided that all senior military officers be appointed by the President, but only with the concurrence of the Senate. As a further check on the abuse of military power at the state level, the Constitution prohibited any state from maintaining troops or warships in peacetime without the consent of Congress, or from waging war unless the state was actually invaded or in imminent danger of invasion.

It is well to note that the Framers arrived at this very important set of decisions concerning military matters with relatively little disagreement. And this lack of contention was echoed in the ratification conventions held in the various states during the next year. The Antifederalists continued to use their supposed concern over a standing army to convince the voters that the proposed Constitution might well lead to the restoration of a European-style government. In fact, a search of the ratification literature reveals little actual discussion of the military subordination issue. At the extreme, one finds Elbridge Gerry, the self-styled "Columbia Patriot," fulminating against the provision for placing the militia, "the bulwark of defence, and the security of national liberty," as he called it, under the national government and, therefore, no longer "under control of civil authority; but at the rescript of the Monarch, or the aristocracy."[20] But in this Gerry exceeded his bounds somewhat. In his eagerness to press the states rights issue, he linked it to the loss of civil authority, knowing full well that the Constitution enshrined the idea of civil authority.

An oblique proof that the Constitution settled the question of military subordination can be read into the *Federalist Papers*. This brilliant treatise on political theory was written by Hamilton, Madison, and Jay with the expressed purpose of defending the Constitution against any arguments that might be advanced by its Antifederalist foes. In one of their rare allusions to civil control of the military, Hamilton argued in *Federalist* No. 28 that "projects of usurpation cannot be masked under pretense so likely to escape the penetration of select bodies of men, as of the people at large." He pointed to the new national legislature as the first line of defense. "They will have better means of information," he pointed out, and "they can discover the danger at a distance." Apprehension on this point, Hamilton observed, "may be considered as a disease, for which there can be found no cure in the resources of argument and reasoning."[21]

Pale stuff, really, and actually aimed more directly at old concerns for standing armies. But these preeminent defenders of the Constitution's never bothering to address the question of civilian control demonstrates conclusively, it seems to me, that they neither anticipated nor received any attacks from this quarter by critics of the Constitution. The inescapable conclusion is that those fears, so constantly raised in the years before the Constitutional Convention, had been stilled by the work of the

Framers.

As one final argument that the Constitution guarantees the subordination of military power, I would mention briefly the actions of the Washington administration as it began to flesh out by law and precedent the principles established in the Constitution. One of the most critical issues facing the first generation of federal leaders was the formulation of a national military policy. With Congress' help, President Washington set important precedents in this area of civil-military relations. Together they determined the size and role of the Regular Army and then resolved the relationship between the states and the national government in dealing with the militia. These decisions had to be made in the context of foreign and domestic policy objectives. They also had to be based on the realities of increasing partisan political activity, since the Constitution explicitly gave the final say to the people, speaking through their elected representatives in Congress, who had to appropriate the funds to pay for troops, guns, and ships. The system they devised—a carefully circumscribed regular military force supplemented by a well-regulated militia—has remained in force for two hundred years.

As rationalists, the Founding Fathers had a profound respect for the appeal of personal civic duty and responsibility. When they approached the question of military subordination, therefore, they focused directly on the individual soldier, mindful of his rights and obligations as a citizen. In the first law written by the new government addressing the raising of troops, the nation's elected leaders called on every officer, noncommissioned officer, and private soldier "who are, or shall be, in the service of the United States" to take an oath, which, with only minor modification in wording, has remained an integral part of the life of every serviceman and woman to this day. In a special way the Founding Fathers made all members of the armed forces their partners when, at the beginning of their military careers, each repeats the familiar words: "I do solemnly swear (of affirm) that I will support the Constitution of the United States against all enemies, foreign and domestic; that I will bear true faith and allegiance to the same."

In taking this oath, servicemen and women not only underscore the country's continuing dedication to the Constitution, but reaffirm that the military forces of the nation are subordinate to civil authority.[22] It is a measure of the success of our system of government, due in no small fashion to the foresight of the Framers, that in taking their military oath, our servicemen and women would help define the essential relationship of the citizen to the Constitution.

Notes

1. Samuel P. Huntington, *The Soldier and the State: The Theory and Politics of Civil-Military Relations* (Cambridge: Belknap Press of Harvard University Press, 1957), 163. Unless otherwise noted, the following paragraphs are based on Huntington's work, especially Chapter 7, "The Structural Constant: The Conservative Constitution versus Civilian Control," 163–77, and Robert K. Wright, Jr., and Morris J. MacGregor, Jr., *Soldier-Statesmen of the Constitution* (Washington: Government Printing Office, 1987), 45–57.

2. These concerns are spelled out in some detail in *Soldier-Statesmen of the Constitution*, 7–11; the influence of these concerns on the development of early military legislation is described on pages 46–57.

3. Ltr., Committee at Headquarters to George Washington, 10 Dec 77, Paul H. Smith, ed. *Letters of Delegates To Congress 1774–1789* (Washington: Library of Congress, 1981), 8:399–400. See also ltr., Francis Lewis to the New York Convention, 30 Mar 78, Henry Laurens' "Notes on Half Pay," 17–21 Apr 78, and especially ltr., Connecticut Delegates to Jonathan Trumbull, Sr., 18 May 78. All in *Letters of Delegates*, 9:354, 426–29, and 707–09.

4. Ltr, James Lovell to Samuel Adams, 13 Jan 77, *Letters of Delegates*, 8:581.

5. Ltr, Laurens to Washington, 5 May 78, *Letters of Delegates*, 9:607.

6. Ltr, Laurens to William Livingston, 19 Apr 78, *Letters to Delegates*, 9:444.

7. The following summary of attitudes towards the Order is based on Don R. Higginbotham, *The War of American Independence: Military Attitudes, Policies, and Practice, 1763–1789* (New York: Macmillan, 1971), 439–41. The quotation is from page 439.

8. As quoted in ibid., page 440.

9. See, for example, Gerry's "Observations on the new Constitution and on the Federal and State Conventions By A Columbian Patriot," 1778, reproduced in Wright and MacGregor, *Soldier-Statesmen* 220–22. See also Richard H. Kohn, *The Eagle and the Sword: The Federalists and the Creation of the Military Establishment in America 1783–1802* (New York: Free Press, 1975), 52–53.

10. The following analysis of the Newburgh affair is based on Kohn's *The Eagle and the Sword*, 29–39, and James T. Flexner, *George Washington in the American Revolution, 1775–1783* (Boston: Little, Brown, 1967), 502–07. The quotations in the following paragraphs are from these two sources.

11. Quoted in Kohn, *The Eagle and the Sword*, 33.

12. Ibid. 37.

13. Don Higginbotham, *George Washington and the American Military Tradition* (Athens, Ga.: The University of Georgia Press, 1985), 37–44. The quotation is from page 38.

14. Richard H. Kohn, "The Greatness of George Washington: Lessons for Today," *Assembly* 36 (March 1978):6–7, 28–29. The quotations are from pages 6 and 28.

15. Washington's Farewell Orders to Armies of the United States, 2 Nov 83. Reprinted in Wright and MacGregor, *Soldier-Statesmen* 191–93. The quotations are from page 192.

16. George Washington, "Sentiments on a Peace Establishment," 2 May 83.

Reprinted in *Soldier-Statesmen of the Constitution*, 193–200. The quotation is from page 194.

17. The following survey of the Convention is based on Wright and MacGregor, *Soldier-Statesmen of the Constitution*, 33–42.

18. Charles Cotesworth Pinckney, quoted in Max Farrand, ed., *The Records of the Federal Convention of 1787* (New Haven: Yale University Press, 1966), 2:335.

19. Gouverneur Morris, quoted in ibid., 2:343.

20. "Observations by a Columbian Patriot," reprinted in *Soldier-Statesmen of the Constitution*, 221.

21. Reproduced in *Soldier-Statesmen of the Constitution*, 231–33.

22. *Soldier-Statesmen of the Constitution*, 46–57.

The Constitution Today and Tomorrow

by

A. E. Dick Howard

I always approach introductions with a certain amount of hesitation, because you're entirely at the mercy of the person who is putting you before a hitherto unknown audience. Your introduction came off flawlessly. It was a contrast to the one I had about a year ago when I was a visiting lecturer for a short time at the University of Hong Kong.

One of my duties was to give a public lecture like this one to a fairly good-size audience. My introducer was the dean of the Law Faculty, a very distinguished scholar. Although his native language was Chinese, he insisted on introducing me in English—I suppose by way of a polite gesture to his American visitor. He had a far more elaborate introduction, with no details spared. Everything I'd ever done was laid out at length before the audience, and he got caught up in the enthusiasm of the moment, and finally he concluded by saying, "Our pleasure at having the distinguished Dr. Howard as our visitor tonight is marred only by our anticipation of what he is about to say." I understood what he was trying to get at, and I appreciated the courtesy, but thank you for not introducing me that way.

It may seem a little bizarre to begin a talk on the U.S. Constitution in Hong Kong, but it's actually not as improbable as it may seem, because one of the reasons I was in Hong Kong was to confer with people who were then at work on a new basic law for Hong Kong, one which will govern the relations of that place with China after 1997.

I also spent some time on that same trip in the Philippines. I was there comparing notes on constitutional revisal with the people who were at work on a new constitution for the Philippines. That was quite a remarkable experience. Some of you have been to the Philippines. You've certainly all followed news from that beleaguered country through the press and television. I was struck by the spirit those people brought to the writing of a new constitution. When I was there, the Constitutional Commission was just beginning its work. Corrie Aquino's People's Revolution was only a few months old, and they were setting out with great boldness with the writing of a new charter. But it was clear that they labored under enormous burdens: Moslem Separationists in the south and Mindanao, a Communist insurgency under arms in the field, and staggering economic problems—the legacy of mismanagement, corruption, and misrule during the Marcos years, an enormous legacy of social, political, and other obstacles and problems.

Now, in the face of all that, one has to pause before being exuberantly optimistic that a new constitution is bound to work. What my travels to Hong Kong and the Philippines taught me is that the nurturing of a constitutional system takes a great deal of work and that one can't really expect constitutionalism, the idea of constitutional rule, to flourish, without regard to the climate or the soil, or the gardener's skill. These things just don't grow of their own accord. They take a great deal of work.

I was also reminded in those travels of the extent to which constitutionalism as we understand it in this country is the exception and not the norm. Most countries in the world, including those that have a piece of paper called a constitution, simply do not enjoy what we would recognize as constitutional liberties. They may have a constitutional regime on paper, but they certainly don't have it in practice.

One is certainly entitled to ask how many of those countries enjoy what we would consider the irreducible minima of a constitutional system—an independent judiciary, a limited government, a rule of law, an enforceable bill of rights, and a truly accountable government.

The fact that we in this country enjoy the blessings of a constitutional system is, I think, not the product of accident, or of nature taking its course. It's the product of a lot of hard work, a travail of experience borne of insights over two hundred years— insights borne as much of mistakes and adversity as of success and triumph. Which brings me to tonight's topic: I speak, of course, as we approach in a few weeks' time the Bicentennial of the drafting of the U.S. Constitution.

None of you, unless you are lying on the beaches of some Caribbean island, will be permitted to escape that fact on September the seventeenth—the anniversary date. Turn off your radios and television and you'll still hear something about it, I'm sure. And I hope you will. I hope you will take note of it.

Eleven years ago we celebrated the Bicentennial of Independence. If I were to pause for a moment and ask people here what they remember of that Bicentennial, what they remember of what happened in 1976, somebody would say, "Well, I remember the tall ships sailing into New York Harbor—what a glorious sight that was." Somebody else would remember the fireworks. There were an awful lot of fireworks that year, more perhaps than at any other time. About that point, we probably would run out of ideas. I'm not sure I could remember anything else about that celebration, except the fireworks and the tall ships.

But if indeed that's all we remember from that Bicentennial, not very much was accomplished. It seems to me that the challenge of the Bicentennial year this time around is to use the occasion for some profound and sober reflection beyond all the hoopla and the pageantry, reflection on the underpinnings, the basic propositions of the American constitutional system.

It seems to me that when one looks at this Bicentennial, the first thing is to demythologize a bit. There's this popular notion—I think many of us share it—that the Framers at Philadelphia were demigods. They were certainly profoundly inspired people, an extraordinary group. But there's this notion that they walked into this steamy room in Philadelphia, and there was this blank slate on which they wrote—stone tablets, more likely—and they produced this remarkable, enduring document as if it were full-blown from the brow of Zeus.

Indeed, the most popular book on the subject is called *Miracle at Philadelphia*. That almost makes you accept a theological notion of the work the Framers did. Well, it was a miracle, but it wasn't a theological miracle. It was a political miracle. It's the kind of miracle politicans on Capitol Hill understand: you know, when you finish rewriting a tax reform bill, and you leave the room, and you say, "By gosh, we did it!" Well, that's how they must have felt on September the seventeenth, 1787: "We did it, we didn't fall apart, we actually were able to get our act together and agree on a constitution."

Now one should not suppose that the Framers in writing that

Constitution somehow drew upon instinct or some sort of abstract principle, abstracted from history and practice. They drew, in fact, upon hundreds of years of Anglo-American constitutional development. These were men who would have been as much at home in the drawing rooms of Paris, or London, or Edinburgh, as in the Tidewater plantations of Virginia or the mercantile offices of Philadelphia or Boston.

These were men who moved on a world stage, and they understood, among other things, the teachings of the British constitution. They were men who knew what Magna Carta was. They knew about the Petition of Rights and the English Bill of Rights. They knew about the seventeenth-century struggles between Parliament and the Stuart kings. They knew how Englishmen in the seventeenth century had worked out, in effect, a constitutional regime, finally bringing William and Mary to the throne in the Glorious Revolution.

They also knew something about the history of their own country. I mean, by 1787 Americans had over a century and a half of something approaching self-government. Obviously, they were colonials; they were subject to rule from Britain; but at least until the 1760s, until the time of the Stamp Act, in a very real sense Americans were largely left free to run their own affairs. So, from the first permanent English settlement at Jamestown in 1607 right up to the eve of Revolution, there was a process of constitutional gestation going on. Americans were really beginning to experiment with the embryonic norms of what we would call constitutional government. And they drew upon that experience at Philadelphia.

They also read books. These were people who, having no television or radio, and not having the distractions that all of us unfortunately are heir to, read Montesquieu. They read John Locke. They read all the other great thinkers of the eighteenth century. They read ancient history and modern history. They drew upon the Whig view of history, that one has to understand what happened in the past to understand one's own time. So when they talked about the lamp of experience, they really knew what they were talking about.

Finally, they drew upon that decade or so of fitful experimentation under the Articles of Confederation and under the state constitutions. One should not overlook the fact that before the U.S. Constitution was written, each of the original thirteen states had a fundamental law of some kind, typically a constitution, written from 1776 onward. A lot of those constitutions were full of mistakes and flaws, and therefore they were the subjects of a learning experience for the Framers at Philadelphia.

So when those fifty-five delegates—and fewer and fewer stayed as time went on—walked into that hall in Philadelphia in May of 1787, they had a vast body of experience, a human experience, upon which to draw. I say all of this because there is a temptation to talk about Philadelphia as if that's where it all began. It didn't begin there. It began centuries before.

There's another error that one falls prey to, and that is to suppose somehow that that's where the commemoration ends, as if to say, "Well, when 1987 is over we can go back to business as usual; we've had our little sermons about the Constitution, and that's it." Well, I would invite you to consider the importance of understanding how the Constitution has unfolded and evolved since 1787. Precisely as there were centuries of experience before that fact, there have been two hundred years of constitutional development since that time.

Consider the contrast between the durability, the longevity, of the American Constitution and the state of affairs in most countries. The vast majority of the countries of the world live under constitutions adopted since 1970. These are young constitutions, and, of course, some of them have never really gone into effect at all; they've been stillborn.

There aren't that many old constitutions around. France, whose revolution occurred only two years after our Constitution was written, has had five republics and seventeen constitutions in two hundred years. I think one would have to be an awfully arrogant Francophobe to argue that somehow the French just can't get it together, that they haven't discovered the secret. In fact, theirs is the typical experience.

Now forgive me if I quote Thomas Jefferson. (You understand that if you teach at the University of Virginia, you are obliged by natural law to quote Thomas Jefferson at least once. I can't go back to Charlottesville unless I have. This is my obligatory Jefferson quote.) For in regard to our own system, Jefferson wrote a letter to a friend in 1816, and in it he said each generation ought to rewrite its constitution and look at it closely and see whether it's really up to date—does it meet the needs of that generation, not of one that's passed? He was writing specifically about the Virginia constitution. But I'm sure, if asked, he would have said, "Yes, I agree, I would apply this principle to the U. S. Constitution, as well."

Most of the American states periodically do revise their constitutions. We rewrote the Virginia constitution in the 1970s. Others have done likewise. But we've never held a convention to rewrite the Federal Constitution in two hundred years. Have we simply ignored Jefferson's advice? What's going on here? Why is it that other countries discard constitutions as if they were outmoded suits of clothes while we hang onto ours?

Well, I wonder whether one might make the case that in fact we have had several Constitutions. Consider the major changes that have taken place since 1787. The ink was hardly dry on the original document before the Antifederalists forced the Federalists, in effect, to agree to a bill of rights. And the adding of the Bill of Rights, of course, was a profound change in the Constitution.

Then one moves through the nineteenth century looking at the opinions of Chief Justice John Marshall, great nationalizing opinions, and they, too, changed the Constitution. One is obliged to take into account the Civil War and Reconstruction, when the roots of the nation were shaken and the Reconstruction Amendments—the 13th, 14th, and 15th Amendments—were adopted. Those Amendments, of course, planted the seed for most of what today is called judicial activism and for much of the power of the modern Congress. In our century one would have to take account of the Wilson administration and, above all, the New Deal, again a profoundly important period for constitutional law. And, finally, one would have to consider the period of the Warren, Burger, and now Rehnquist Courts, the Supreme Court as it has become in the last twenty-five years—a period of extraordinary explosive litigation in that tribunal. Maybe if you take each of those chapters in our Constitution's history, maybe we, like the French, have also had five republics, rather than one.

Well, what this does, it seems to me, is raise a couple of questions about how Americans use their Constitution. One of those questions, I think, would be to consider how we've evolved from a Constitution whose preoccupation was with limits on government—what Hugo Black used to call the thou-shall-nots of constitutional law—toward a more affirmative view of government, where entitlements come to take their place alongside prohibitions. It also calls into play what the pundits and the commentators would call "the litigious society."

You can't open the newspaper without one more op ed piece on how Americans love to go to court. We love to litigate in this country. I mean, all of you have been a party to a lawsuit or have a friend or a member of the family who's been in a lawsuit. You know, when people say "there ought to be a law," my response is that there already is one on almost any subject you can name. I think our national motto perhaps ought to be, "See You in Court."

You hear people complaining about judges doing too much—we all do that—and yet Americans are the first ones to put those complaints aside and go to court and sue. People say, "I'm going to take it all the way to the Supreme Court." How often do you hear that? Well, what this means is that we live in an age and in a country, America, in which people, lawyers and their clients, have an uncommon ability to take ordinary, prosaic garden-variety disputes—the sort of disputes which even thirty years ago nobody would have thought of suing over—and not only make lawsuits out of them but turn them into constitutional questions.

I remember a recent case, for example, in Richmond, Virginia, where I grew up, of a high school trombone player. The kid missed band practice one day, and the director of the band said that because he had missed practice he would have to sit out the next Saturday football game when the band was marching at halftime. The kid would have to sit up in the stands. Well, you know what it's like to be fifteen and be so shut out. That's a traumatic experience. You're the object of mockery when all of your friends are down there marching and you're not.

Well, not only was it traumatic, his parents said, it was also a federal case. And so they went to the Federal District Court in the Eastern District of Virginia under the Civil Rights Statute, Section 1983, complaining that the due process clause had been violated by the band and by the school system. A lot of money was spent on that litigation, and I am happy to say that the judge threw it out, as I think he should have done. Now the county is suing the parents to recover lawyers' fees, and so you see, this is ongoing litigation. Dickens talked about unending lawsuits in nineteenth-century England. We have our examples today. What we have is a Constitution which has somehow become a vehicle for social, political, economic, and moral issues of all kinds—race, criminal justice, abortion, you name it. They all come before the Supreme Court. The Constitution is, in effect, a mirror of the

American mind.

You've all heard the old saying that the Constitution is what the judges say it is. I think that's often said rather cynically. My reformulation of that statement is that the Constitution is what people ask the judges to say it is. The judges can't decide a case until someone comes to the court and asks for a decision, and we oblige the judges left and right. We go to court taking every issue we can think of, asking for its judicial resolution.

Now, where does this take us when we think about the Constitution's Bicentennial? Let me suggest several directions for our trying to extract some worthwhile lessons from the Bicentennial year. The first suggestion I would make is to use the Bicentennial to do some learning about our own history. The Framers understood the places and uses of history. We should use the Bicentennial to learn something about the roots and the origins of the American constitutional system, both before and since 1787.

Secondly, I would submit that we ought to use the Bicentennial to appreciate the force and place of ideas in constitutional government. It's very easy to debunk ideas and say, "Well, people are not moved by ideas; they're moved by economics, by pocketbook issues." But he who concedes that, I would say, concedes the ground to the Marxists, because that's their thesis—that it's only economics that matter. I don't think the American system or American history supports that conclusion. I think the Framers thought that ideas mattered, and I think we should take that view today as well.

Now, I admit that maybe I've been brought to that point of view by my mentor Hugo Black. He thought ideas mattered. When I reported for work in Hugo Black's chambers at the Supreme Court, I was just back from Oxford, and nobody thinks better of himself than someone who's just back from Oxford. So the first thing Hugo Black did was shake his bony finger at me and say, "Howard, when you're working on my opinions, I want you to write not in the language of Oxford but in the language of your country's forebears." Good advice. And then he turned to the subject of ideas and history, and he started pressing books on me.

Hugo Black, when he came to the U.S. Senate from Alabama, from politics down there, really hadn't had much of a classical education, and he felt the want of that. So he set out to read all the books he thought he should have been asked to read as a student. He read ancient history—Thucydides, Tacitus, Herodotus, all that sort of thing. He read English history of the nineteenth century—Gibbon, Carlyle, et cetera. He educated himself through these books.

Well, when he had law clerks, he wanted them to read the same books. So at the end of a long working day, when all I wanted to do was go home and think about nothing serious and turn on the television, he'd give me a copy of Tacitus or Thucydides and I'd be expected to take it home and read it. And then, of course, the next morning he'd ask me about it, and that was the worst thing about it. So I had to read the wretched books. Well, I learned the hard way, but I learned through a justice who I think was privy to the world view of the Framers. He, like them, understood the place of ideas, and I hope we might think about that during the Bicentennial.

Let me suggest further that we use the Bicentennial to assess the health of the American constitutional system. By that, I mean, in particular, the institutions of constitutional government. How fair is the separation of powers, checks and balances, federalism? I mean, we've had on television this summer something approaching a medieval morality play, as all the heroes and villains came and went during the Iran-Contra hearings. Like a lot of people, I found myself glued to the set half the time just to see who would be next. But behind all of that drama lay serious questions about the separation of powers, about the powers of the President, the powers of Congress, about accountable government. These are the kinds of questions I think Americans ought to be thinking about during the Bicentennial.

I would suggest also that during this Bicentennial we consider the Constitution as a social document, as a mirror of American aspirations. If the Constitution works well, one thing it must do is unleash the talents of a people. That was surely what the Founders had in mind: that the government should have the power and energy to deal with national problems, but that it should stand aside from individual initiative, so that people could get on with the business of living and seeking the good life. We certainly ought to be asking whether the constitutional system, as it works today, permits people to unleash their talents regardless of their religion, their race, or their ethnic origins.

I hope also that we would look to the Constitution for a sense of shared values, of community, because we are a very diverse nation. We march to the sound of many drummers. One would hope that the Constitution might be common ground where people could come together under one flag.

And finally, let me suggest that I can't think of a better textbook than the Constitution, because it's a textbook that one uses to teach the basic values of citizenship—how it is that the principles of free government are passed along from one generation to the next, and how it is that a free people govern themselves under conditions of ordered liberty. In particular, it provides a way in which we accommodate the competing values in our society—the tensions, for example, between liberty and equality, between the public sector and the private sector, or the tension between, if you like, heritage and heresy. It's a way to accommodate the value of tradition on the one hand with the need for change and adaptation on the other. This kind of transition is what most countries don't succeed in making peacefully. They go through war, revolution, dictatorships, and so forth. We've somehow managed for two hundred years, through the Constitution, to make these changes in a peaceful fashion.

Now, as we mark this Bicentennial Era, I invite you to consider the mixed experience of other nations. You have very few countries—England is certainly one of them—who enjoy constitutional liberties. You have a much larger group of countries—surely those behind the Iron Curtain for the most part—in which there may be a constitution in the formal sense, but not a system we would recognize as being genuine constitutionalism. And, thirdly, we have countries like the Philippines where, with a certain amount of luck and pluck, they may pull it off.

Certainly, I think the Constitution ought to be considered as being more than simply an instrument of government. It's not the property of lawyers and judges and technicians. It really is a document which creates a continuing seminar in self-government, an ongoing dialogue among people over the nature and ends of their institutions of government.

Now, I'm casting about for a theme to sum all of this up. You're expecting Thomas Jefferson. Well, I've given you my one Thomas Jefferson quote. James Madison, the father of the Constitution, comes to mind, of course, but let me borrow my concluding theme from one of the opponents of the Constitution, George Mason. Some of you live out in Fairfax County, and, as you may know, George Mason went to the 1787 Convention as a delegate from Virginia. But he was one of the three delegates who refused to sign the document. He went back to Virginia and was an Antifederalist opponent of the Constitution in the Virginia ratifying convention.

In 1779 Mason, Patrick Henry, and others were very powerful in their opposition. History tends to write off the Antifederalists as just sore losers, as small-minded reactionaries. In fact, it was thanks to the Antifederalists that we got the Bill of Rights. And George Mason was one person who understood what constitutions were all about. Eleven years before the Federal Convention at Philadelphia, he was the principal architect of the first declaration of rights and constitution of any of the states—the one written in Virginia in May 1776.

In that document there's language which is still in the Virginia constitution, and it reads, as follows, that "no free government, or the blessing of liberty, can be preserved to any people, but by frequent recurrence to fundamental principles." A frequent recurrence to fundamental principles: it strikes me that this language from George Mason is a suitable theme to adopt for the Bicentennial of the Constitution.

Question-and-Answer Session

Question: I wonder if you would care to comment on the perception of the Founders as to the appropriate role of the President and the Senate in the selection of justices; how those perceptions have been expressed over the years; and what difference, if any, you see Judge Robert Bork making on the Supreme Court.

Howard: Let me break that apart into two questions, if I may. One question on the respective role of President and of Congress in the selection of justices, and what difference will Bork make?

This raises that intriguing question about original intention. What did the Framers really mean? Nothing is more elusive than to try to nail down with some definitiveness what the Framers really thought. For one thing, of course, there was no official journal of the Federal Convention. James Madison kept notes, which he suppressed for the rest of his life. They were published posthumously.

So it takes a fair amount of indirect speculation to suppose what kind of accommodation the Framers really had in mind. It turns, of course, on the constitutional language, which says that the President shall nominate justices or officers with the advice and consent of the Senate. Now, that phrase "advice and consent" is freighted with ambiguity. It's not self-revealing language at all, and it's the result of a process in which the Framers, in working out the Constitution's language, actually went through several stages to resolve the whole question of executive and legislative power. That's the larger backdrop of it.

I'm sure the Framers must have had in mind, in part, the experience of the states, because most of the states had begun with arrangements of essentially legislative supremacy. Under the colonial regime, the colonists identified executive power and judicial power with the Crown, and therefore they were objects of suspicion. The legislature represented the people.

As of 1776, that made a lot of sense. Eleven years later Americans had come to realize that the problems often lay with the legislative branch and not with the executive, and so the trend was toward trying to create, as Hamilton put it, energy in the executive, and therefore to give the President more power. It seems to me that what they set out to do was to create a system in which it wasn't perfectly clear what role was to be played by those two branches. I like to think—and on this I may be quite wrong— that there was a certain air of calculated ambiguity in language such as "advice and consent," that Madison and his contemporaries at Philadelphia understood that writing a constitution was a great experiment, and that, therefore, they would simply write it, painting in fairly broad brush strokes and leaving it for experience to work out the details. I think "advice and consent" is an example of that.

My hunch is—and the evidence on this is, I think, somewhat scanty—that they neither intended the President to have free play, unfettered power to choose, or they would have left out the language altogether, nor did they intend stalemate, i.e., that each branch should exercise, both of them, unfettered judgment. I think they had in mind that separation of powers had to be tempered by ways to keep the system working, and they didn't mean for nominees to be continually shot down.

What I think has evolved, and this may be closer to the mark, is a practice in which what I guess I would call a lightly resting presumption attaches to the President's nominee. I think the modern sense of it is that if a nominee is professionally qualified and a man or woman of personal integrity, it is still appropriate for the Senate to play a role beyond that of simply rubber stamp, but that it would take a very powerful case, a persuasive case, to overturn the President's nominee. I think that has come to be the unfelt, perhaps unarticulated, sense in the matter.

Now, as to what difference Judge Bork would make, I think more than the Antonin Scalia nomination last year; and I think that is why there's so much electricity over this particular nomination. I mentioned morality plays, the Iran-Contra hearings. We're going to have another morality play starting September the fifteenth. When the Senate Judiciary Committee starts quizzing Judge Bork, you will not recognize him. He'll be painted on the one hand as the greatest jurist since Hammurabi and on the other hand as a demon reincarnated, a man prepared to strip the Constitution and leave it in pieces, strewn about us. These both will be caricatures, of course.

The question really is, what difference will he make? Let's assume that Bork is confirmed. I think you will see immediate differences in a few areas—church and state, where there are many five-to-four decisions; affirmative action, surely an early area to see some change; and perhaps some aspects of abortion cases. The so-called social issues are areas where I think Bork's hand will be felt. But I'm not sure that Mark Cannon really intends that I should look at it case by case. I think what he has in mind is what difference would Bork make jurisprudentially. And there I think we may enter into an era that we haven't seen for the last twenty-five years, that is to say, the emergence of uncommonly able people on the Court, people who really do have the stuff, the understanding of the jurisprudential questions. Bork would be that kind of a judge.

No one, no matter how much he dislikes Bork, has doubted the man's intellectual firepower. This is a man of remarkable intellectual achievement and insight. What he would do is clearly sharpen debate, focus issues. I think the Court would tend to be more polarized, at least at the outset. Namely, instead of seeing a somewhat floating voting pattern, as it often was in the 1970s and early 1980s, we would tend to see two camps on the Court, with issues laid out rather more starkly than they have been in recent years.

Question: Referring to something you mentioned before, I'm rather interested in the public perception, that if there were to be a constitutional convention of the states, it would turn somehow into pandemonium and chaos and they would literally tear the Constitution apart. Since the Constitution provided this mechanism as an alternative to amendments, I'm puzzled as to why there seems to be this fear, especially since whatever this convention would do, it would still have to be ratified by three-quarters of the states, as any amendment or change to the Constitution would be. I'm just wondering if you have any particular thoughts.

Howard: You know, one is free to speculate at large because we've never had a convention since 1787, and I think one reason you hear the arguments that you've alluded to is that in constitutional theory a convention is the people, the sovereign people met in convention, and that legislative bodies like Congress can't really cabin the authority and power of a convention.

But you rightly point out that even though the convention may decide to disregard its instructions and propose all manner of amendments on a wide range of subjects, any amendment to the Constitution still has to be approved by three-quarters of the states. That surely is the safety valve.

I think the reason why one worries, or why you hear these worries expressed, is that the only historical precedent that we have is the Philadelphia Convention, at which those delegates clearly defied their instructions. They were there to revise the Articles of Confederation; they simply decided more than that was needed, and they wrote a new Constitution. But, of course, once again it had to be approved by the requisite number of states.

I suppose they could change the ground rules in a new convention. I mean, they did that at Philadelphia. The Articles required unanimity to change that document; the Framers of 1787 said nine states would do. I suppose one could imagine a scenario in which a new convention said that instead of three-quarters of the states, 51 percent of the states would do to adopt a new Constitution. I could imagine all of that in theory, but I can't imagine anything like that in actual practice. Let me say that I think your question will remain hypothetical, because I think it's not likely we'll get enough states calling for the convention. Even if two additional states do—I think they're two short of a call—I could well imagine Congress laying the calls for a convention side by side and discovering that they used different language, with a lawyer then saying, "Well, these don't look like the calls for the same convention, and therefore we don't have to call one." If Congress doesn't call a convention, I can't imagine that a federal judge would mandamus the Congress to call a convention. I think that would be the end of it.

Question: Professor, would you share some of your personal views on the tug-of-war between the original intent of the Constitution and the Constitution as a dynamic vehicle subject to constantly. . . .

Howard: I love the way people tonight are asking all these simple questions that yield very short answers. You obviously like wordy law professors who talk a lot. No one, of course, has not been hearing about this debate.

Let me compliment Ed Meese for one particular thing. Aside from how one feels about his speeches on original intention, he has popularized the debate. I mean, it used to be that this was the sort of question only academics and professionals and judges cared about, but now people at large hear about and have some sense of the debate, and I think that's wonderfully healthy.

I made a comment a moment ago about how elusive it was to pin down what the Framers meant by "advice and consent." The problem is that this may be a slight skewing of one's vision, for the majority of questions are not that difficult. The Supreme Court is asked to decide 5,000 cases a year. It only writes opinions on 150 of them. The vast majority of legal questions are pretty well settled by the time they get that high up and almost everyone, left or right, then says, "Yes, that's the answer."

Many other questions simply require you to read the language of the Constitution; I mean the steps through which a bill becomes a law are precisely the steps that they were in 1787. It's very clear what you have to do to pass a bill.

But there are a handful of genuinely ambiguous phrases—"due process of law," "equal protection" of the laws, "cruel and unusual punishment"—and that's where the fuss lies. If you think about the cases that upset people, the cases that really traumatize commentators of left or right, they tend to be the social issues that are decided under those few ambiguous clauses. And there, I think, original intention is a difficult argument to make. The first question is: Whose intention are we talking about?

Let's say it's the Fourteenth Amendment. Do we mean the intention of the members of Congress who voted for that Amendment? Do we mean the votes of the various state ratifying bodies who were called to pass on the Fourteenth Amendment, or do we mean the understanding of the people at large who were informed about the issue at the time? First you have to identify who we mean. And then if you can get over that hurdle, you have to decide what counts as evidence for original intention. How would you go about deciding what they thought? You can't exhume people and ask, "Were you thinking about desegregated schools in 1868 when you passed the equal protection clause to the Fourteenth Amendment?"

All of this is very difficult, because the language they used had already evolved. The due process clause traces back at least to the fourteenth century. If you follow that phrase from the fourteenth century through the nineteenth century, five hundred years, you watch it constantly taking on new meaning in an evolving fashion.

I think at bottom what makes constitutional interpretation so difficult, and what makes the debate so sharp over original intention and the living Constitution, is the tension between two essential approaches to thinking about the Constitution. One is a belief in text, and this would be understood in theological circles: that words set down in scripture or holy text must mean something. That's one approach to Biblical or other theological interpretation. That gives a certain security. For one thing, it means that you can bind judges and other people who interpret the text. If you have something that has a fairly secure meaning, then you're not so likely to be bandied about by particular judges. Their subjective judgments are not going to be as important. And so that search for security is one side.

On the other side is the understanding that there has to be sufficient adaptability, because no one can ever foresee all of the crises and problems that will come up. It's very instructive to read the tracts and pamphlets which were written at the time of the Revolution attacking British policy. When Americans were complaining that the British were violating the rights of Americans as Englishmen under the colonial charters and under the British constitution, they staked their cases on written documents like

Magna Carta and at the same time also on natural law, in the same resolutions. I've read hundreds of them, and they almost all have these different levels of argument, and then the writer of the tract will say that it doesn't matter which plane of argument you're on, since it all amounts to the same thing: We have rights which the British aren't recognizing.

So, in that first decade or so leading up to Philadelphia, Americans became conditioned to thinking, as lawyers often argue today, on different levels of abstraction—natural law, written documents, and so forth. We began on a note of ambiguity, it seems to me, and therefore the debate continues.

This all seems a very circular way of answering your question, but I think it means that you simply can't give any final answer to where the truth in that argument, if there is truth, actually lies.

Question: You expressed the hope at the outset that Americans might take something more than fireworks and tall ships away from this Bicentennial. I wonder if you could say a little about some of your favorites in the literature on the Constitution and on the American system?

Howard: The text of the Constitution, absolutely first and foremost. It's appalling how many people have not read a fairly short document. I mean, I'd sit down and read the thing, and I'd think about its language and about when different parts of it come into play and how they relate one to another. I'd begin with text.

Let me say that the suggestions I'll make are in no particular order, and they might not be definitive, and I might leave the stage and say, "Oh, how could I have forgotten such and such, but I'll toss out two or three ideas."

The *Federalist Papers:* It seems to me that the *Federalist Papers* may be the most important single American contribution to political theory. Now, one need not read every paper, but I think one would want to single out *Federalist* No. 10 and some of the others that are seminal documents that have profound influence quite beyond our own country. And so I'd say that the *Federalist Papers* would be number two.

Number three, I think, would be something on the historical origins, of which I've had something to say tonight. Something like Gordon Wood's book, *The Creation of the American Republic, 1776–1787,* would be a very good study. It'd take you especially through the founding period.

And fourthly, I think I'd want a book on the Philadelphia Convention. Why not *Miracle at Philadelphia?* It's a very readable book, but one has to be cautious with the title, that's part of the mythologizing. Nevertheless, I recommend the book.

I would then read about the Antifederalists. I mentioned George Mason tonight. Herbert J. Storing wrote a book called *What the Anti-Federalists Were For.* It's a very short book, a hundred pages maybe—very readable. It will give you a real sense of why adopting the Constitution was not simply an open-and-shut case. There was a lot of concern about it, and the Antifederalists were very prescient. They raised questions which I think one still ought to be worried about today.

Then I would read something about the place of the Constitution in American culture, and I recommend Michael Cammens' *A Machine Which Would Go of Itself,* published within the last year or two. It's about the iconographic uses of the Constitution.

Finally, I'd certainly read—and here there are a lot of books you could choose—something about the current scene, the original intention debate, that kind of thing. I'd try to read something good on the Supreme Court. If you want a really tangible look at a case going through the Court, it would be hard to improve on Anthony Lewis' *Gideon's Trumpet.* It was written back in the 1960s, but the case is about the right to counsel, and I think it's a vivid account of a case moving on through the Court.

Now, I have neglected some very good books that I'm sure just haven't come to mind. But let me simply suggest you ought to begin squarely with history and then move on to some of the books on the more contemporary scene.

Question: Would you give us, in your opinion, the reason for the notoriety that was attached to George Mason?

Howard: For one thing, he was kind of a crotchety fellow. He comes down to us as not being mellow or affectionate to people. I think he suffers from the syndrome that those who wind up on the losing side of historical arguments get a bad press. It's as if they just didn't get it right, and as if not understanding what would happen later meant they were wrong in the first place. I think that's the problem with George Mason, Patrick Henry, and all the other Antifederalists. But I really think they were uncommonly insightful people. Mason also disappeared from the public scene after 1788. He didn't linger on to make a mark in national government, as some of the other Framers of his generation did.

I've said a lot about the Antifederalists tonight. They really ought to be honored next year when we look at the Bicentennial of Ratification. In 1987 I would honor Madison and the Federalists and the Framers. Next year I would move on to think about the Antifederalists, such as George Mason, and then compare the two, because both groups have something to teach our time.

Contributors

Dan Higginbotham, Professor of History, University of North Carolina, is an expert on the American Revolution and on civil-military relations. His works include *Daniel Morgan: Revolutionary Rifleman* (1961); *The War of American Independence* (1971); *Atlas of the American Revolution* (1974); and *Reconsiderations on the Revolutionary War* (editor, 1978).

Robert A. Rutland, Editor in Chief, Papers of James Madison, University of Virginia, specializes in the history of the early national period. His works include *Birth of the Bill of Rights, 1776–1791* (1955); *The Papers of George Mason* (1970); *James Madison and the Search for Nationhood* (1981); and *The Papers of James Madison*, vols. 8–14 (1973–82).

Richard Buel, Jr., Professor of History, Wesleyan University, has concentrated on the Revolutionary and early national periods of American history. He is the author of *Securing the Revolution: Ideology in American Politics* (1972); *Dear Liberty: Connecticut's Mobilization for the Revolutionary War* (1980); and, with Joy Buel, *The Way of Duty: A Woman and Her Family in Revolutionary America* (1984), as well as other works.

Jack P. Greene, Andrew W. Mellon Professor in the Humanities, Johns Hopkins University, specializes in the study of the colonial and early national periods of American history. His works include *The Diary of Colonel Landon Carter of Sabine Hall, 1752–1778* (1965); *The Ambiguity of the American Revolution* (1968); and *Great Britain and the American Colonies, 1606–1763* (1970).

Allan R. Millett, Professor of History and Director of the Program on International Security and Military Affairs, Mershon Center, Ohio State University, is a nationally known military historian. His works include *The General: Robert L. Bullard and Officership in the U.S. Army* (1975); *Semper Fidelis: The History of the US Marine Corps* (1980); and, with Peter Maslowski, *For the Common Defense: A Military History of the United States of America* (1984).

Lawrence Delbert Cress, Professor of History, University of Tulsa, is an expert on the early national period of American history and the early militia. His works include "Radical Whiggery on the Role of the Military: Ideological Roots of the American Revolutionary Militia," and *The Army and the Militia in American Society to the War of 1812* (1982).

William A. Stofft, brigadier general, United States Army, is the Army's Director of Management and former Chief of Military History. His works include (with Charles Heller) *America's First Battles 1775–1965* (1986).

A. E. Dick Howard, is the White Burkett Miller Professor of Law and Public Affairs at the University of Virginia. An authority on constitutional law, Professor Howard is the author of *The Road from Runnymede: Magna Carta and Constitutionalism in America* and *Commentaries on the Constitution of Virginia*.

www.ingramcontent.com/pod-product-compliance
Lightning Source LLC
Chambersburg PA
CBHW080246290526
45790CB00005B/1726